SHADOW SIDES

SHADOW SIDES

The Revelation of God in the
Old Testament

Dr H.G.L. Peels

PATERNOSTER
PRESS

First published in 2003 by Paternoster Press

09 08 07 06 05 04 03   7 6 5 4 3 2 1

Paternoster Press is an imprint of Authentic Media,
PO Box 300, Carlisle, Cumbria, CA3 0QS, UK
And PO Box 1047, Waynesboro, GA 30830-2047, USA
www.paternoster-publishing.com

British Library Cataloguing in Publication Data

A catalogue record for this book is available from
the British Library

ISBN 1-84227-198-9

Cover design by FourNineZero
Printed in Great Britain
by Cox and Wyman Ltd., Reading

Contents

Contents

Preface

Who is God? At the Sea of Reeds Israel sings, full of respect, 'Who among the gods is like you, O LORD? Who is like you – majestic in holiness, awesome in glory, working wonders?' (Ex. 15:11). In the Old Testament this question, 'Who is like you?,' is often heard. People ask it again and again when they are impressed by God's power and majesty. The song at the Sea of Reeds is sung after the destruction of the Egyptian army that wanted to eliminate Israel. God had intervened in a powerful way and delivered his people. The context of the question 'Who is like you?' testifies to God's destroying retribution, which causes terror and fear, shivering and trembling.

The way in which the Old Testament speaks about God may be alien and even frightening to the average reader of the Bible. The God who hides himself in anger, who in jealousy executes judgement, who repents and takes revenge, before whose holiness people fall to the ground as dead – who is he? Many people do not really know how to handle these 'shadow sides' of the Old Testament revelation of God. These things may even become an obstacle to faith. Is this the same God as the One who is our salvation, the Lord, our light and life?

This book is written primarily for all those who stumble over questions like these. It is meant to help them read the Bible 'from within', and to listen better to the message about the living God. The book is suitable not only for personal use but also for discussion in house groups etc. At the end of each chapter there are five questions which aim to stimulate reflection. Students and ministers may find things which require further investigation; to that end a short bibliography is appended to each chapter.

I wholeheartedly wish that the readers will share my experience whilst looking for nuggets in the word of God, which is 'more precious than gold, than much pure gold' (Ps. 19:10) – that, while reading with an open mind, surprising light is thrown on the so-called 'shadow sides' of God's revelation in the Old Testament. How rich the Scriptures are and how rich they make us!

H.G.L. Peels
Apeldoorn, October 2002

1

God's Revelation in the Old Testament

1.1 Introduction

The importance of the subject

The subject of this book fixes our attention on a question which is of great relevance to our personal faith as well as to the confession of the church: Who is God? Much depends on how this question is answered. Whom do we deal with when we close our eyes and pray? Whom shall we meet when we close our eyes forever and die? Who is he who created us, who keeps our life in his hands, who speaks to us in the Bible? Who is the One who gave the law, our daily guideline? Who is the One who gave effective power to the Gospel, which we daily hold on to? We hardly need to explain that the issue of 'shadow sides in the Old Testament revelation of God' will not only cause exegetical and biblical-theological problems, but also touches the heart of the Christian faith, which in Old Testament terminology is the fear of the Lord. True faith in God includes the element of knowledge and of trust (Heidelberg Catechism, question and answer 21). If the knowledge of God revealing

himself in his word for one reason or another is some-
how inadequate or partial, the ability to trust him and
his promises will suffer from this as well. Unknown,
unloved.

Definition of the problem

Everyone who reads the Bible is regularly confronted
with the problem that the Old Testament sometimes
speaks about God in such a different way from the New
Testament. In the Old Testament there are passages
which frighten us in such a way that the difference from
the New is almost too great to be reconciled. Some examples may clarify this point. Forty-two boys who are
mocking and scolding are torn into pieces by two she-
bears, because God hears Elisha's prayer calling down a
curse (2 Kgs. 2:24). But the Son of the same God, the Lord
Jesus Christ, did not curse when they mocked and scold-
ed him. He did not threaten them, when he suffered
(1 Pet. 2:23). At God's command whole nations of
Canaan were wiped out in the time of Joshua and the
Judges. Yet Jesus says: 'You have heard that it was said,
"Love your neighbour and hate your enemy." But I tell
you: Love your enemies and pray for those who persecute you, that you may be sons of your Father in heaven.
He causes his sun to rise on the evil and the good, and
sends rain on the righteous and the unrighteous' (Mt.
5:43-45), and: 'Are not two sparrows sold for a penny?
Yet not one of them will fall to the ground apart from the
will of your Father. And even the very hairs of your head
are all numbered' (Mt. 10:29-30). 'O God who avenges,'
the writer of Psalm 94 cries out (v. 1). 'God is love,' the
apostle John confesses (1 Jn. 4:8,16).

Many of us cannot help feeling that the image of God
in the Old Testament sometimes seems to have features

which are more human than spiritual, more unreasonable than understandable. God is walking in the garden of Eden in the cool of the day (Gen. 3:8). Smoke rises up from God's nostrils, consuming fire comes from his mouth by which coals are set alight (Ps. 18:8). When Uzzah wants to prevent the ark from falling, his death is the immediate result of God's anger (2 Sam. 6:7). God not only punishes the one who is guilty, but also his family (in the case of Korah, Dathan and Abiram in Num. 16), and even the whole people (in the case of Israel at Ai in Josh. 7). God's clothing is stained and red from Edom's blood where he trampled nations in the winepress (Is. 63:1-6). The God of Lot does not say anything when Lot wants to give his daughters to men on the street in order to save his guests (Gen. 19:8), or later on when Lot is drunk and commits incest with these girls (Gen. 19:30-38). The God of Jephthah is silent when this judge sacrifices his only child after he has made a silly promise (Judg. 11:29-40). The story of the shameful act at Gibeah is disgusting (Judg. 19).

What a difference there seems to be with the message of the New Testament. God is light and there is no darkness in him, says the apostle John (1 Jn. 1:5). Hear how Paul sings of God's mercy and love for men (Tit. 3:4)! The life of the early church (Acts 2:41-47) is rather different from the way people lived in the times of the Judges and Kings. How are these things to be reconciled? If there are that many 'shadow sides' in the Old Testament revelation of God, can human beings ever be certain about him? Will faith in God therefore always keep a margin, a dark side or 'shadow side', of doubt and even fear? Can we really count on the Lord? Is the One who reveals himself in the Scriptures, in both the Old and New Testaments, indeed one and the same, just and merciful?

Purpose

In this book we will reflect on the above-mentioned issues. Our aim is modest; we can only make a limited investigation in which we deal with a small part of the larger issue of the relationship between the Old Testament and the New. From the Scriptures we hope to gain some insight into the specific character of the Old Testament revelation of God, the Lord, who reveals himself but also hides himself. He can be envious, he sometimes repents, he avenges himself in anger and fury. He is the holy God to whom poets and prophets fiercely pray to intervene and destroy the enemy. Our purpose is to throw more light on these 'shadow sides' of the Old Testament revelation of God. The questions we meet will draw us to the heart of what the Scriptures tell us about the Lord God.

First, however, it must be clear how we read the Old Testament, which 'reading glasses' we need. This determines everything. It is clear that none of us can read the Bible with a blank mind. Everybody has their presuppositions, whether they say so or not, what they intuitively like or dislike. Therefore we first need to give an account of the way in which we listen to the Bible. We will look at some false tracks first. Then we will try to understand how the Old Testament wants to be read. The testimony the Bible itself gives to us is decisive.

1.2 False tracks (a): a truncated canon

An unbridgeable gap

In the early years of church history people already had an eye for the questions and problems we have just indicated. In the middle of the second century AD the notorious Marcion declared that he could no longer accept the Old Testament as normative. The God of the Old Testament is a severe Creator-God, he stated, a God of law, justice, revenge and war. Jesus has come to deliver humankind from the regime of this God. The Father of Jesus, the God of the New Testament, is a totally different, 'strange' or 'alien' God, a God of love and mercy. An unbridgeable gap separates the Old Testament from the New. Marcion despised the Old Testament as Scripture of the church. In addition, he started to remove from the New Testament everything which reminded him too much of the Old. He depleted the Gospel of Luke and purged the letters of Paul (whom he thought to be the apostle *par excellence*) of 'legalistic' elements. A 'truncated' canon was Marcion's solution for screening the biblical image of God from any 'shadow side'. Until now many have followed in his footsteps. We mention some famous German scholars like Friedrich Schleiermacher, Albrecht Ritschl, Adolph von Harnack, Friedrich Delitzsch and Emanuel Hirsch.

The practice of Bible reading

In the tradition of the church throughout the ages the 'solution' of Marcion's truncated canon has never gained a legitimate place. Yet this kind of idea may certainly occur in the minds of those who read the Bible today, though in most cases this is hidden. The Old Testament is a nice old book, some say, it is interesting for historical and cultural research, etc., but how do you handle it in the practice of the life of the church and in personal faith? Many people like to read the New Testament much more than the Old. And when they read the Old Testament, they prefer the well-known parts of Genesis and Exodus, Samuel and Kings, Isaiah and the Psalms.

This means that in daily practice they actually handle a 'canon within the canon', though of course no one will openly and readily admit this. However, we must not underestimate how this range of thoughts may affect many people and how it brings about insecurity. It may hinder and even block a wholehearted commitment to God.

1.3 False tracks (b): a dismantled canon

Modern views

A second false track is the 'dismantled' canon, as we would like to characterize the way of thinking of some modern theologians. Marcion stated that a great deal of the Bible did not contain any divine revelation. These modern theologians state that the Bible does not contain any divine revelation at all. The Bible is the result of human experience and insights alone. If that were the case, it is not surprising that the Bible contains images of God which contradict each other. This would be no problem, because in that way of thinking the Bible does not speak the final word in our reflections on God. The Bible is an inspiring book, but it is not normative.

As an example we mention the names of two Dutch scholars, whose work has been translated into English and therefore has a wider influence. The Old Testament scholar Cas Labuschagne (University of Groningen) considers the Bible to be a documentation, embedded in history, of testimonies of faith and of the insights of human beings in the times of the Bible. As such it is a human product. The same sort of subjectivism characterizes the views of Harry Kuitert, who taught Dogmatics at the Free University of Amsterdam. He considers the Bible to be 'the classical expression of the

Christian picture of God'. He does not like the dogma of inspiration: he re-evaluates the concept of revelation as a collection of Christian truths about God. They have not come down from heaven, but they are characterizations of God and his salvation originating in human beings and expressed in human language. They are based on the experience of many generations before us. There is no guarantee, they do not carry a divine stamp or seal by which one knows that they are good. Kuitert pleads for the use of the Bible as a kind of breviary: we can reflect on it, but it is not meant to prescribe how we must think. In my opinion, this dismantles the Holy Bible as a normative canon. The 'problem of the shadow sides' is no problem any more. Bible reading is without obligations and this solves each tension.

The Reformed doctrine of the Bible

In a Reformed interpretation of the Bible we cannot give up the principle that the Bible is more than human words. The great discovery of the Reformers of the living heart of the Bible was that it is the very word of God by which the Lord himself speaks. Today this is as relevant as it was in those times. Of course there are human experiences and insights in the Bible, but they are embedded in and taken up in God's revelation. The God who speaks gives us a thorough impression of the mighty and all-embracing salvation in Jesus Christ, by the testimony given by the Holy Spirit. In this way we know from within that this word has authority. The way in which the Bible testifies about itself makes us accept that all Scripture that we received in this form is the word of God without any distinction. It requires a reverent and true openness to listen. The way in which the Lord Jesus and the apostles deal with the Old Testament points us in the right direction.

1.4 The testimony of the New Testament

The New Testament on the Old

In the reverent way in which the authors of the New
Testament deal with the Old, it is concluded that the
Bible, written by human beings, is to be understood
essentially and primarily as the word of God. Words
from the Old Testament are referred to as words from
God (Acts 13:35-36; Heb. 1:5-13) or from the Holy Spirit
(Acts 1:16; Heb. 3:7). God spoke through the prophets
(Heb. 1:1); the Spirit of Christ testified through their
words about what would happen to Christ (1 Pet. 1:11).
These Scriptures testify about Christ (Jn. 5:39), who came
to fulfil them completely (Mt. 5:17-18). The Scriptures
cannot be broken (Jn. 10:35). The apostles' sermons are
full of quotations of the Old Testament and references to
it. The Old Testament, which Paul refers to as the 'very
words of God' (Rom. 3:2), is the basis and the source of
the New Testament and is accepted as the word of God
in its entirety.

The New Testament on the God of the Old Testament

Nowhere do the New Testament authors appear to have
any problems with the revelation of God in the Old. On
the contrary: to them the Father of Jesus Christ is none
other than the God of the covenant at Sinai. We wonder
whether the New Testament authors did not see the
'shadow sides' of the Old Testament revelation of God.
Were they not shocked by the blood, by the violent acts
and the sometimes humanly disgraceful abuse in the Old
Testament? How is it possible that they apparently did
not feel any inconsistency between their God and
Saviour, who is love, and the God of revenge in the Old

Testament? How is it possible that they easily quote psalms with a curse like Psalm 69? Were they too naive, or is it possible that we read the Old Testament through tinted glasses?

A historical reading

Reading the Bible with tinted glasses can make things more difficult. Perhaps many of the problems that modern readers experience when reading the Old Testament, and the objections to the Old Testament revelation of God in particular, stem from poor knowledge of the Scriptures and from reading them too superficially. In particular there may be a wrong view of the relationship between the Old and the New Testaments. The basis of all this is often an a-historical reading of the revelation of God in the Bible. The Bible is not a Christian Qur'an, not a ready-made heavenly book. When God reveals himself to us, he does not just give us a range of truths about himself in a dogmatic system which is timeless. If that were the case, the Bible would indeed contain contradictory views. Yet it wants to be read as a historical book. God speaks and acts and this is how he is part of history. The notion of history is essential to a right understanding of the biblical revelation of God.

There are two concepts which need to be distinguished: the history of revelation and salvation history.

1.5 The history of revelation

Progress in revelation

In due course God made himself known more and more in history. He did not tell us everything at one time.

There is a progress in his revealing himself and so there is a history of revelation. An important verse is Hebrews 1:1: 'In the past God spoke to our forefathers through the prophets at many times and in various ways, but in these last days he has spoken to us by his Son...' We can also think of the parable of the unfair tenants in the vineyard in Matthew 21:33-44. In the Old Testament itself the progressive revelation is indicated, as in Exodus 6:3: 'I appeared to Abraham, to Isaac and to Jacob as God Almighty, but by my name the LORD I did not make myself known to them.' The concept of a progressive history of revelation figures regularly in Reformed confessional documents (e.g. Heidelberg Catechism, question and answer 19, and Belgic Confession of Faith, article 25).

We quote two theologians who explain the notion of the history of revelation in striking words, using the metaphors of an increasing light and a sculpture. John Calvin writes: '...at the beginning when the first promise of salvation was given to Adam (Gen. 3:15) only a few slender sparks beamed forth: additions being afterwards made, a greater degree of light began to be displayed, and continued gradually to increase and shine with greater brightness, until at length, all the clouds being dispersed, Christ the Sun of righteousness arose, and with full refulgence illumined all the earth...' (*Institution* II.10.20). The Dutch Old Testament scholar Theodoor Vriezen expresses this in the following way in his *An Outline of Old Testament Theology*, Oxford 1958: 'Like an artist who works on his intractable material with his chisel and a steady hand and who sees the image slowly take shape and emerge from the shapeless mass of stone, God has worked on the "image of God" in mankind. In the Old Testament it emerges rather in the manner of some of Rodin's sculptures where the work of art is still

interfused with the material from which it has been created. In the New Testament the work of art is completed
and the conception that God has of and for man, the
Image of God, stands out clearly in Jesus Christ' (p. 17).

The relevance of perceiving the history of revelation

Why is the perception of the history of revelation so
important for the comprehension of the Old Testament
preaching about God? Because in this way readers of the
Bible become aware of the fact that they should not just
put all sorts of texts from the Old and the New
Testaments on one and the same level. In an earlier stage
of history we cannot expect the same sort of clarity we
have in the New Testament. In his revelation God sometimes joins in current opinions and insights (that is what
Calvin calls 'accommodation'). God may change these
concepts, however – he 'baptizes' them, as it were, and
later on in history he gives more insight. We will
illustrate this briefly in dealing with three examples, considering the issue of

a. God and the gods
b. God and evil
c. God and suffering

a. God and the gods

From the whole of Scripture we know that there is only
one God. Polytheism is a human invention. Yet in the
Old Testament there are all sorts of texts which suggest
that the existence of other gods is a reality. Thus
Jephthah tells the kings of Ammon: 'Will you not take
what your god Chemosh gives you?' (Judg. 11:24) and
Naomi says to Ruth: 'Look . . . your sister-in-law is going
back to her people and her gods. Go back with her'

(Ruth 1:15). In 1 Samuel 26:19 David tells of other people who would like to get rid of him by telling him: 'Go, serve other gods.' Asaph sings a song about God, who stands in the council of the gods and gives judgement among them (Ps. 82). Only in a later stage of history does the issue become clearer, and the prophets mock other gods (the first one to do that is Elijah in 1 Kgs. 18:27; later in particular Jeremiah and the prophet of Is. 40-48). The history of revelation has already gone through many centuries before we hear: 'I am God, and there is no other; I am God, and there is none like me' (Is. 46:9).

b. God and evil

What is the relationship between the acts of God and evil? In former times it is explained as a strong and direct relationship. For example, in the story of the census in 2 Samuel 24 God is said to have incited David against Israel (v. 1). In later times there is more clarity about this: in the parallel text of 1 Chronicles 21 we read that it was Satan who incited David against Israel. The story of 2 Samuel is retold in 1 Chronicles 21 with the help of the proclamation in the book of Job: God allows Satan to act.

c. God and suffering

Of course the moving story of the sacrifice of Isaac in Genesis 22 is horrifying. How much Abraham suffers! He loses everything he has. And does God not cause it? How capricious this God seems to be when he asks for a human sacrifice, even though it later appears to be intended as a test. This is incomprehensible as well. How unpredictable the God of Genesis 22 seems to be – if one only looks at that chapter. Only in a wider perspective of the history of revelation does one get another view. The God who requires this sacrifice is the same God who gives everything through his Son, who is the sacrifice of his love.

Old Testament believers receive more and more insight into who God is. Yet we must not state too readily that Jeremiah knew God better than, for instance, Noah, for even in Noah's time, at the beginning of the world's history, God opened up his heart. We can say, however, that Jeremiah knew God in a deeper way. What was there in an implicit way, yet hidden, now becomes more open. In Noah's time we can compare the knowledge of God with the sunlight shining through a small window into a loft. In Jeremiah's time it is the sunlight (the same light) shining through a big window into a living room. What we applied to God's revelation we can also apply to a lot of other things in the Old Testament. When we read the Old Testament, we must constantly take into account the history of revelation, which is progressing, widening and deepening. Knowing this is indispensable for a right understanding of Old Testament ethics (what about the polygamy of the patriarchs and kings?), of what the Old Testament says – or rather of why the Old Testament is silent – on life after death (did Old Testament believers expect it or not?), the position of the nations, etc.

1.6 Salvation history

God's 'way' in dealing with the world

If we want to understand the revelation of God in the Old Testament (in the strict sense of revelation about God himself) in a better way, we need to say a bit more. The fact that revelation is progressing clarifies several aspects, but does not yet fully explain all the differences in the image of God which we first find in the Old Testament and then in the New. Of equal importance to the interpretation of the differences between the two

parts of the Bible is the view of salvation history. By this
we mean the specific way in which God has dealt with
the world to deliver his people from darkness into light.
This 'way' of God passes through several covenants: the
covenant with Adam in paradise, the covenant with
Noah, the covenant of grace with Abraham and
with Israel at Sinai, the covenant with David, and the
new covenant in Christ. If we do not pay attention to this
history of salvation and of covenant and how God and
human beings act, if we just combine all sorts of sayings
about God in the Bible and compare them with one
another, we do not do justice to the biblical revelation of
God. We will end up with contrasting images of God.

Narrowing and widening

We will look at salvation history with a bird's-eye view
and use the words 'narrowing' and 'widening'. Salvation
history starts off with the whole range of people: God
created heaven and earth and wants to have the earth
filled with life. This universalist beginning, however, is
narrowed after the increasing sinning and faithlessness
of humans (Gen. 3-11) into a particularist intensification.
Nations are spread around the world (Gen. 11) and God
calls Abraham (Gen. 12). Through him God chooses one
people, yet in the meantime he is still considering other
nations: '...all peoples on earth will be blessed through
you' (v. 3). Through Israel God wants to realise his purpose for the world. Israel, however, is going the same
way: it is not loyal to God. The situation narrows even
more. From Israel as a whole there is a line drawn to
Judah, the chosen tribe, and finally to David, who in a
very special way is the chosen one among his brothers.
All this leads to the coming of Jesus Christ, who is the
true man of God, the true Israel, the true David, the

second Adam. After he fulfils his work on the cross and in the resurrection, salvation broadens again, for this is made possible. Through Pentecost salvation flows into the world and passes the borders of Israel (compare Peter's vision in Acts 10). Therefore, when we try to find an answer to the question who is God?, we must constantly bear in mind this way of salvation. We cannot loosen God's acts from this history, which may be compared to an hour-glass for measuring time: from broadening via narrowing to broadening again.

Israel as an 'experimental garden'; the time of patience

It is important to bear in mind constantly the special position of Israel in salvation history. The old dispensation knew of a specific concentration on Israel; in that period salvation was very real and earthly and nationally based. Israel was, so to speak, the experimental garden of the world. This nation represented in one part the whole of the world. The king of this nation was God. He wanted to live with them and to reflect his holiness among all of them. There was no room for anything impure, imperfect, or untrue. In a certain way, the whole life of Israel was on edge. The greatest happiness, which is being the people of God, should be paired with the greatest commitment: to be holy. *Noblesse oblige*: 'Be holy because I, the LORD your God, am holy' (Lev. 19:2). In this very special framework of salvation history we therefore need to put the Old Testament proclamations about the sometimes incomprehensible anger of God, about the expulsion of Canaanite peoples, about very strict punishments, about an extremely precise legislation concerning clean and unclean, etc.

But what do we actually read in the Old Testament? That all this fails time and again. Repeatedly Israel is

faithless and breaks the covenant. It is the history of an
increasing contest, a battle, a struggle. The further you
get, the two things become clearer. In the first place,
human beings do not manage, for they are hopelessly
unfaithful. In the second place, God does manage, for he
continues to be faithful in judgement and grace. The
more salvation history proves human impotence and
guilt, the more it becomes clear who God is in his awesome holiness, in his anger in which sinners cannot exist,
and in his love and patience which we cannot understand. In this way the Old Testament prepares the way
for the New and shows us why it was necessary for
Christ to come into this world. Through his coming it
became fully clear who God is: 'Anyone who has seen
me has seen the Father' (Jn. 14:9). On the cross of
Golgotha it becomes clear to the utmost who God really
is. There anger and love are one.

   In the person and work of Christ the Kingdom of God,
which in the Old Testament was about to 'fail' because of
human sin (that of Israel and of the nations), is firmly
established. In the Old Testament the expectation of the
Kingdom of God meant both judgement and salvation:
judgement for the godless, salvation for the righteous.
That is why John the Baptist does not understand at all
what Jesus is doing: where is the axe at the root of the
tree, where is baptism with fire (Mt. 3:11 and 11:3)?
Judgement is executed, but ... in Jesus himself. His
humiliation is an exaltation which causes God's
Kingdom to break through in a definitive way. Today it
is present, it is here *already*, though *not yet* in a perfect
and undisturbed way. Now is the time for a worldwide
proclamation of the Gospel. The godless are not judged
– not yet. Let them grow up together with the harvest,
Jesus says (Mt. 13:24-30, 36-43). God's judgement has
now been executed in Christ in a principal and anticipa-

tory way. The final phase of history is dominated by the tension between the 'already' and the 'not yet' of God's Kingdom. We live in the period of God's patience: 'He is patient with you, not wanting anyone to perish, but everyone to come to repent-ance' (2 Pet. 3:9). That patience brings a delay, but it does not cancel judgement. That is why we read relatively less about God's judgement in the New Testament than in the Old.

Final remarks

As a summary we can state that the so-called 'shadow sides' of the Old Testament revelation of God can only be understood in the right way in the light of the history of revelation and that of salvation. This does not mean, however, that it is easy to answer all questions. On the contrary, the more we listen to the testimony of Scripture, the more we realize that the proclamation about the living God constantly gets away from our (theo)logical systematizing. Often the questions are too difficult, too high above us. Our considerations and 'solutions' fall short. God is always greater. The medium by which we can embrace the word of God is not our rational intellect but a heart that echoes. This way of understanding holds the future: 'Now we see but a poor reflection as in a mirror; then we shall see face to face. Now I know in part; then I shall know fully, even as I am fully known' (1 Cor. 13:12).

1.7 Lasting value of the Old Testament revelation of God

The Old Testament as a blossoming flower

One question still remains: when in Christ God revealed himself fully, when Christ is the purpose and the centre

of the history of salvation, why do we still need the Old
Testament? When the sun shines, why should we keep
the shadow? Yet God's revelation in Christ can only be
understood in the context of the whole Bible. Just as the
New Testament shows us the purpose of the Old, so the
Old Testament shows us the richness of the New. After
Christ has come, the Old Testament is not a withering
flower without any value. It is a flower which through
his coming is in full blossom and shows us its great
beauty. There are four reasons why the revelation of God
in the Old Testament is indispensable.

Indispensable

In the first place the revelation of God in the Old
Testament is indispensable because of its *height*. Even
more than the New Testament, the Old proclaims God in
his exaltedness, his glory, his holiness, his majesty and
highness. God is the Creator, the one who shapes the cos-
mos. He is a great King, the Judge of the world, the
awesome Lord. He goes on in majesty, incomprehensi-
bly, saving in his power and supremacy. In the Old
Testament we learn to take off our shoes like a little child,
just like Moses. Like Isaiah we realize we have unclean
lips, like Job we put a hand on our mouth.

In the second place the revelation of God in the Old
Testament is indispensable because of its *depth*. How
deeply the Old Testament searches the love of God! We
can think of the frequently used metaphors of marriage
and upbringing (prophets like Hosea, Jeremiah, Ezekiel).
God acquires Israel as his bride. Even after she commit-
ted adultery many times God still says: 'Come back to
me!' As a loving father/mother God took Israel in his
arms, fed them, taught them how to walk (Hos. 11). And
how deeply the Old Testament searches God's anger!

This is the frightening anger of God, which cannot tolerate the damage to his creation, the defilement of his holiness and the attack on his people. God does not allow darkness to speak the final word – but he intervenes. God cannot be mocked, because of his very love of human beings and creation. The proclamation of judgement by the prophets is one great call to repentance and life. God is angry, because he loves in a holy way.

In the third place the revelation of God in the Old Testament is indispensable because of its *width*. The New Testament concentrates on the blast of trumpets at the coming of the Kingdom, the reconciliation and the salvation, but the Old Testament has a wider perspective. In it we see that God is Lord in every area of life. All aspects of human life are glimpsed: the government, the economy, politics, sexuality. Nothing is excluded from the relationship with the Lord God.

In the fourth place God's revelation in the Old Testament is indispensable because of its *length*. It tells us a long history which is a mixture of salvation and doom. In the Old Testament we see God's way through the history of the world and the nations, in grace and judgement. We get to know him in his patience and particularly in his faithfulness. He keeps his promises, he lives up to his word in his speaking and acting through the ages, in his reacting and persevering in an inexhaustible way. We hear about God's plan, God's way, God's work. Over the course of the Old Testament we learn how to believe and hope in a far-reaching way.

The height of the Old Testament portrait of God prevents us from self-exaltation; it teaches us how to kneel down. The depth of the Old Testament prevents us from cheap grace and teaches us the seriousness of sin as well as the ardour of God's love. The wideness of the Old Testament prevents us from spiritualization and urges us to live before God in all areas of life. The length of the Old Testament prevents us from short-sightedness and teaches us how to hope in persever-ance; to hope for the God of Abraham, Isaac and Jacob, Moses and David, Elisha and Jeremiah, the God and Father of our Lord Jesus Christ, the trinitarian God who is the same and will be, yesterday, today and for ever.

Questions

1. Which elements in the Old Testament revelation of God present you with problems and how do you deal with them in the practice of Bible reading, prayer and meditation?

2. Which false track do you think is a more serious fail-ure, that of the 'truncated' canon or that of the 'dismantled' one?

3. What exactly is the difference between 'history of revelation' and 'salvation history' (or 'redemptive history')?

4. How can we explain that in the Old Testament there seems to be a lack of view of resurrection and afterlife in the world to come?

5. A Chinese pastor once said: 'Reading the Old Testament is like eating lobster: much shell, little meat.' What are the consequences of such an under-estimation of the Old Testament for the way in which we relate to the Lord in faith?

Bibliography

Baker, D.L., *Two Testaments, One Bible. A Study of the Theological Relationship Between the Old and New Testaments.* Revised and Enlarged Edition, Leicester 1991.

Childs, B.S., *Biblical Theology of the Old and New Testaments. Theological Reflection on the Christian Bible,* London 1992.

Hasel, G.F., *Old Testament Theology: Basic Issues in the Current Debate,* Grand Rapids 1991.

House, P.R., *Old Testament Theology,* Downers Grove 1998.

Kuitert, H.M., *Het algemeen betwijfeld christelijk geloof. Een herziening,* Baarn 1992 (German, *Ich habemeine Zweifel,* Gütersloh, 1993).

Labuschagne, C.J., *Wat zegt de Bijbel in Gods naam?,* Den Haag 1977.

Rendtorff, R., *Theologie des Alten Testaments. Ein kanonischer Entwurf.* Zwei Bände, Neukirchen-Vluyn 1999 and 2001.

VanGemeren, W. van, *The Progress of Redemption: The Story of Salvation From Creation to the New Jerusalem,* Grand Rapids 1988.

Van Ruler, A.A., *Die christliche Kirche und das Alte Testament,* München 1955 (= The Christian Church and the Old Testament, Grand Rapids 1971).

2

The Mystery of God in the Old Testament

2.1 Revelation and mystery

Richness and limitation of the revelation

The Old Testament testifies to the self-revelation of God. The Lord reveals himself in a variety of ways: in history, in nature, in dreams, in visions, through outward means like the Urim and Thummim or the ephod, and in particular through his word. To human beings this revelation, of which we have a firm record in the Bible, is incredibly rich. God's word in human language can be heard and understood and is, according to the psalmist, '...more precious than gold, than much pure gold... sweeter than honey, than honey from the comb' (Ps. 19:10). For this word is 'a lamp to my feet and a light for my path' (Ps. 119:105). If we did not have this word we would not be able to get to know God. By his revelation he visited humankind, he broke the silence and searched for a relationship. We can learn from the Scriptures in a completely reliable way what God is really like.

Yet we always need to keep in mind that God in his inmost being is hidden from us (we use the words 'inmost being' in a reverent way). Revelation is limited by the limitation of human language, which matches our human comprehension. Revelation takes place within the structure of the reality of this earth. It is the only possible way. Yet how can human concepts and categories tell us completely who God is? God's revelation tells us much about him, but not everything. God's being is much greater, richer and more wonderful than our human comprehension can ever grasp. We must keep this well in mind when we are reading the Bible and meet the so-called anthropomorphisms – that is, human ways of speaking about God (God is walking, he is roaring with anger, he delivers with an outstretched arm, he descends to look at man, he equips as a warrior, he repents and is jealous, etc.).

Limits of revelation

Not only is the revelation limited because of our human comprehension, God himself draws a line to his revelation. No one can ever claim to know everything about God. One only knows just a little, as much as God wants to reveal. No one can take the Bible and say: 'Now I understand God and I can describe exactly how he is.' This reminds us of a little boy at the beach who got some water from the sea in his bucket and proudly told his parents: 'Look, I've caught the sea!' God is and will forever be the Holy One, the incomprehensible, essentially hidden God. We can only know him in so far as he allows us to.

The limitation of God's revelation is clear from the Old Testament. 'The secret things belong to the Lord our God, but the things revealed belong to us and to our children for ever...' (Deut. 29:29; cf. also Job 28). What is a human being compared to God? Less than a drop of water in a bucket, a little dust on a scale: 'The Lord is the everlasting God, the Creator of the ends of the earth' (Is. 40:28). 'As the heavens are higher than the earth, so are my ways higher than your ways and my thoughts than your thoughts' (Is. 55:9). Human thinking or guessing will never be able to reduce God's incomprehensibility, his sacrosanctity or hiddenness – he 'who alone is immortal and who lives in unapproachable light, whom no-one has seen or can see' (1 Tim. 6:16). In his revelation God made himself known to human beings in a completely trustworthy way. He is not different from the God we get to know in the Bible, yet he does not lose himself in it. He is always greater.

In the Old Testament a sign of this is God living in the 'holiest of holies', in the inaccessible dark part at the back of the temple. The shape of the 'holiest of holies' is a cube, a symbol of perfect space. No one was allowed to enter this part except for the high priest who came once a year at Yom Kippur. In the world of the Old Testament this was a unique event. The temples of the Ancient Near East also contained a kind of 'holiest of holies', which was called the 'cella'. Although this was considered to be the place where the gods actually lived in the centre of the temple, the priests were always allowed to enter it. They were responsible for providing the gods daily with food, clothing and anointing.

In the Bible the Israelites were forbidden to make an image, which is striking. God cannot be portrayed and no one is allowed to try. God's revelation is like a bright light, but it does not remove the hiddenness of God which is essential to his being.

Hiddenness and God's hiding

We must make a distinction between God's essential hiddenness as described above and the fact that God may hide himself in the history of the people of Israel and in the daily life of pious people. For whatever reason God can withdraw deliberately from the life of Israel, he can hide his face. This leads to a frightening darkness and silence, and it is usually a reaction to the acts of man. We therefore cannot speak only of a hiddenness which belongs to God's essential being, but must also speak of him deliberately hiding himself as a reaction to what humans do. In the following part we will deal with God's hiding himself.

2.2 The experience of the God who hides himself

Gottesfinsternis and theological research

The experience of the God who hides himself or who seems to be absent is a reality to numerous modern people. In the 1950s the Jewish scholar Martin Buber put forward the term *Gottesfinsternis* (*Finsternis* meaning 'darkness'). Following his lead many theologians and philosophers have given an outline of the basic experience of modern human beings in which God is absent, but the questions have just increased. Buber stated that God lives behind a wall of darkness. Human beings do not see him any more, neither do they experience him. In the confusion of what happens in the world, God has become the totally Absent One, the great Unknown. Many people still believe in a supreme being, but he does not really speak to modern man, for people today no longer consider him to be a person. In recent years theological research has increasingly dealt with all these questions.

Possible causes

Of course many have tried to indicate possible reasons for this 'darkness' in people's experience of God. One may look in different directions. The enormous speed at which the process of secularization has developed is linked with the spiritual and moral disorientation of a society which gave itself too much in terms of a materialistic way of living and a scientific way of thinking. Furthermore, the world is disillusioned because of the two World Wars which took place and perhaps the threat of a third one in the future. Potential environmental disasters are ticking like time bombs. The optimism of the nineteenth century has long since vanished. More than ever, humankind is aware of the chaotic and capricious nature of the history of nations and humankind and of the amazing amount of injustice and meaningless suffering on earth. Last but not least, we must remember the advancing power of unbelief (cf. Lk. 18:8). Doubting God and his hand in history, doubting God and his hand in nature, doubting God and his hand in suffering – all these things (and much more) have deeply imbued our culture and society. No wonder that many complain about the lack of an experience of God.

The issue is not new

The experience of the absence of God is, however, not a novelty. There have been periods before in the world's history in which humans asked in despair: 'Where is God?' We may think of the so-called 'insane' fourteenth century, full of massive destruction, socio-economic chaos and spiritual undermining, when Islam advanced, and the pestilence mowed down like a scythe a third of the European population. There was also despair in the time of Augustine at the decline of Rome as capital of the empire of the world. For centuries Rome had been the heart of an inviolable empire which reigned over the earth. Yet the Eternal City turned out not to be everlasting when Alaric and his Goths captured it in AD 410 and when the Vandals led by Gaiseric plundered the city in AD 454. We may even return to earlier times. In the Bible, particularly in the Old Testament, people frequently ask for God, who seems to be absent and who hides himself.

2.3 The Old Testament on God's hiding

Terminology and metaphors

How is this theme expressed in the Old Testament? Let us first notice the most important expressions which are used. The most important word is obviously 'to hide'. Thirty-two times the Old Testament speaks of God hiding or concealing his face or himself. Did Israel not get to know the Lord as a God who makes his face shine upon them or who turns his 'face' towards them (Num. 6:25-26)? A second expression is: 'to be far away.' 'Why, O LORD, do you stand far off? Why do you hide yourself in times of trouble?' the author of Psalm 10 cries out (Ps. 10:1). Israel had got to know the Lord as a God who is 'near' (Deut. 4:7 and Jer. 23:23). A third word is to 'be silent' or to 'be deaf'. 'To you I call, O LORD my Rock; do you not turn a deaf ear to me. For if you remain silent, I shall be like those who have gone down to the pit,' says the beginning of Psalm 28. Was the Lord not the one who hears (cf. Ps. 34:6,17)? Besides the words mentioned above (to hide, to be far, to be silent), the Old Testament often uses the terminology of 'forsake', 'forget', 'reject', 'to cast away from', 'to turn his face away'.

God's hiding can also be indicated by the use of several metaphors. An example is Psalm 18:9, 11: 'He parted the heavens and came down; dark clouds were under his feet ... He made darkness his covering, his canopy around him – the dark rain clouds of the sky.' Jeremiah prays: 'O Hope of Israel, its Saviour in times of distress, why are you like a stranger in the land, like a traveller who stays only a night?' (14:8). Psalm 44 uses the metaphor of sleeping: 'Awake, O Lord! Why do you sleep? Rouse yourself! Do not reject us for ever' (v. 23).

Questions and results

The use of words like 'how long', 'when' and 'why?' is characteristic of the language used in Old Testament prayers. Very frequently these questions occur in the book of Psalms. Apart from the passages above we mention two more examples: 'How long, O LORD? Will you forget me for ever? How long will you hide your face from me?' (Ps. 13:1); 'How long, O LORD? Will you be angry for ever? How long will your jealousy burn like fire? Why should the nations say, "Where is their God?"' (Ps. 79:5,10). In these words we hear despair and desolation.

So it is clear that the Old Testament believers had the experience of a God who hides himself; they suffered from it intensely. The author of Psalm 30 (vv. 7-9) prays: 'O LORD, when you favoured me, you made my mountain stand firm; but when you hid your face, I was dismayed. To you, O LORD, I called; to the Lord I cried for mercy: What gain is there in my destruction, in my going down into the pit? Will the dust praise you? Will it proclaim your faithfulness?' Job even feels threatened by God: 'Why do you hide your face and consider me your enemy?' (13:24). A striking example is Psalm 104:29: 'When you hide your face, they are terrified; when you take away their breath, they die and return to the dust.' The fact that God hides himself harms life and brings about the reign of darkness. When God makes his face shine upon the people (Num. 6:25) life is without fear and worries. Yet if he hides himself there is an 'eclipse' and the powers of illness, plague and death have free play.

2.4 Some examples

Deuteronomy 32

We will now deal with some Old Testament passages in which God's hiding plays an important role. In the first place there is Deuteronomy 32, the famous song of Moses. Some have called it a summary of prophetic theology. This passage is very important within the Old Testament and its influence can be noticed in many other Bible passages. Moses wrote it at God's command and taught it to Israel, to be sung from generation to generation as a witness against them (Deut. 31:19). This is the way it may have functioned in Israel's cult and worship.

Verses 1-6 are an introduction in which the theme of God's loyalty and Israel's faithlessness are indicated. In the following passage (from verse 7 onwards) the issue is elaborated by referring to history and to what happened between God and his people. This leads to verse 18: 'You deserted the Rock, who fathered you; you forgot the God who gave you birth.' The remaining part (from verse 19 onwards) sings of judgement. It says what God had already mentioned in Deuteronomy 31:16-17, when he announced his hiding as a judgement on Israel's religious adultery. Thus Moses sings in 32:19-20: 'The LORD saw this and rejected them because he was angered by his sons and daughters. "I will hide my face from them," he said, "and see what their end will be; for they are a perverse generation, children who are unfaithful."' God withdraws and leaves Israel to their own devices. Their faithlessness will return to them as a boomerang. Later on, Isaiah 64:7 will express the same idea as follows: 'No-one calls on your name or strives to lay hold of you; for you have hidden your face from us and made us waste away because of our sins.'

Job

The book of Job is a moving witness to the experience of God's absence. While his friends are making theories about the incomprehensibility of God (34:29; 36:26; 37:5,23), Job suffers in an existential way because of God's hiddenness. Robbed of everything, even of his children and his health, he sits on the ground and does not understand. God is absent: 'But if I go to the east, he is not there; if I go the west, I do not find him. When he is at work in the north, I do not see him; when he turns to the south, I catch no glimpse of him' (23:8-9, cf. 9:11). He experiences God's absence as the unjust action of an enemy: 'His anger burns against me; he counts me among his enemies' (19:11, cf. 13:24 and 33:10). Job uses very strong words about God: 'God assails me and tears me in his anger and gnashes his teeth at me; my opponent fastens on me his piercing eyes ... All was well with me, but he shattered me; he seized me by the neck and crushed me. He has made me his target' (16:9 and 12). All this is highly moving: we hear a little human being bowed down in the dust, a man whose voice cries out to heaven without result. No answer is given – not yet.

Psalms

A third example comes from Psalm 88, the darkest of all the psalms. It has an almost paradoxical tension. The author calls to God in verse 1, to the Lord, the 'God who saves me'. And he reproaches the same God that he has

put him in the deepest darkness (v. 6), that he has overwhelmed him with all the waves of his anger (v. 7).
People around him consider him to be dead, no one cares
about him (vv. 4-5). In fact he is a living dead. In verses
10-14 the questions accumulate and lead to the important question in verse 14: 'Why, O LORD, do you reject me
and hide your face from me?' The final verse of the
psalm speaks of 'darkness'. The author cries out all his
distress to God, but there is no light. The worst thing is
that this God is the God of the covenant. Is he the One to
rely on? Can he be trusted? Throughout all the questions
in the book of Psalms the righteousness of God is at
stake. Isn't he the living One? Is his Name not called on
by the people: YHWH – 'I am who I am'? When a person
believes, 'Your love, O LORD, reaches to the heavens,
your faithfulness to the skies' (Ps. 36:5), it is so much
harder in distress and pain, when heaven seems to be
closed and there is only a cold silence that cries out the
absence of the God of the covenant.

Prophets

A fourth and final example comes from the prophets. In
Isaiah 1:10 Judah and Jerusalem are addressed as
'Sodom and Gomorrah'. It appears that the people only
want to serve God outwardly. They are extremely religious, but behind that there is not much which is good.
Israel's religion has become a plastered grave. There is
nothing more disgusting to the Lord:

> Stop bringing meaningless offerings! Your incense is
> detestable to me. New Moons, Sabbaths and convocations –
> I cannot bear your evil assemblies. Your New Moon festivals
> and your appointed feasts my soul hates. They have become
> a burden to me; I am weary of bearing them. (vv. 13-14)

But their practice of prayer is the most shocking (v. 15):

> When you spread out your hands in prayer, I will hide my eyes from you; even if you offer many prayers, I will not listen. Your hands are full of blood...

God hides himself as a reaction to and a judgement on Israel's aversion to him. The beginning of the great book of Isaiah therefore cuts deeply:

> Hear, O heavens! Listen, O earth! For the LORD has spoken: 'I reared children and brought them up, but they have rebelled against me. The ox knows his master, the donkey his owner's manger, but Israel does not know, my people do not understand.' Ah, sinful nation, a people loaded with guilt, a brood of evildoers, children given to corruption! They have forsaken the LORD; they have spurned the Holy One of Israel and turned their backs on him. (vv. 2-4)

God abandons Israel, because Israel abandons God.

2.5 Reasons for God's hiding in the Old Testament

A response to sin

When we search for reasons for God's hiding in the Old Testament we should do so carefully – on the one hand because we are never able to check God's works and ways, and on the other hand because the Bible does not speak about his hiding everywhere in the same way. In the passages we dealt with from Deuteronomy 32 and Isaiah 1 we can certainly state that, particularly in the announcement of doom by the prophets, God hiding himself is clearly related to Israel's sins. Whoever leaves God, God will leave him. Whoever hides from God, God will hide from him. This is clear from Isaiah 57:17: 'I was enraged by his sinful greed; I punished him, and hid my face in anger, yet he kept on in his wilful ways.' In a straightforward way Jeremiah states that God has hidden his face from Jerusalem because of the wickedness of its inhabitants (33:5). In this case God's hiding means literally that his anger is present and therefore he cannot help or hear. These are the words of the prophet in Isaiah 59: 'Surely the arm of the LORD is not too short to save, nor his ear too dull to hear. But your iniquities have separated you from your God; your sins have hidden his face from you, so that he will not hear' (vv. 1-2; cf. 54:7-8). The actual problem is not *God's* absence, but the absence of man.

Not only in the prophetic preaching but in the psalms as well we regularly find the mature understanding that God's hiding is related to the guilt of man. We mention for instance Psalm 89, where the author cries out in relation to the Davidic throne and crown (v. 46): 'How long, O LORD? Will you hide yourself for ever? How long will your wrath burn like fire?' In the same psalm Nathan's prophecy from 2 Samuel 7 is quoted: 'If his sons forsake my law and do not follow my statutes, if they violate my decrees and fail to keep my commands, I will punish their sin with the rod, their iniquity with flogging...' (vv. 30-32). There is a relationship between God's absence and the sins of David's sons. Psalm 79 is no different. 'How long, O LORD? Will you be angry for ever?' (v. 5). God seems to be absent, so the heathens say: 'Where is their God?' (v. 10). At the same time the author prays in verse 8: 'Do not hold against us the sins of the fathers...' In Psalm 69 two prayers coincide: on the one hand in verse 5, 'You know my folly, O God; my guilt is not hidden from you', and on the other hand in verse 17, 'Do not hide

your face from your servant; answer me quickly...'
Compare also Judges 6:13 after 6:10: Gideon cannot
find a reason why God has left his people and hidden
himself (v. 13), but there clearly is a cause, as the
unknown prophet had indicated: 'But you have not
listened to me' (v. 10).

Cause unknown

Yet not everything is said. In the Old Testament there is
also the possibility of the closure of heaven remaining
an enigma. Often the Old Testament believers really do
not know why God seems to be absent and why he
remains silent. That happens despite a clear need for
God's revelation: the people's distress, the mockery of
the heathen, the threat of death when one will not be
able to praise God any more – and yet God remains hidden! The clearest example of this is obviously the book
of Job. To Job's friends there are no enigmas. In fact
they had only one explanation of Job's suffering and
God's absence: Job's sins. His friends therefore had just
one solution to offer Job: to humble himself and repent
(8:5-10; 11:14-20, etc.). They repeated the same statement again and again: believers will be blessed and
godless people be punished (5:2-7; 8:11-22; 11:10-20,
etc.). Job himself could draw the same conclusion, but
he resists! In 33:9 he says literally: 'I am pure and without sin; I am clean and free from guilt.' Job suffers and
struggles with his God. And even when he finally finds
God again, the Lord has not given him any explanation.
God reveals to Job a little part of his majesty and that is
sufficient. The fact that God's hiding was related to the
battle in the heavenly realms is something that the Bible
reader knows from Job 1 and 2, but Job has never
known.

2.6 The Old Testament and modern man

A similar experience?

We now return briefly to the comparison of the Old Testament and the situation of modern man. We realize that it may be extremely difficult to compare the experience of God's absence in modern times immediately with that in the time of the Bible. Great indeed is the difference between the living environment of the people of Israel, who lived in a specific relationship with God in a theocracy, and modern humankind in a secularized society. Yet it is not impossible to draw a parallel. The experience of God's hiding does not only play a role in the Old Testament, neither is it exclusively modern. Through all ages human beings have – to a greater or lesser extent – experienced God hiding himself. Each time life on earth became unbearable and heaven seemed to be as impenetrable as a nuclear bunker, questions went upwards in an urgent, threatening or appealing way.

A different experience

At the same time there are enormous differences, of which we mention three. First, in the time of the Bible people would admit that through the absence of God something of his anger was executed. Nowadays this understanding is mainly absent. We do not hear much about 'guilt' towards God. Modern human beings are not afraid of God any more – they rather shape him the way they want, if indeed they have not yet declared him to be dead. But at the same time people lift their accusing finger towards heaven ('Where is God?') and not towards themselves. Second, the search for God in the Old Testament differs in accent and character from that

of modern human beings. In the Bible people struggle
with God himself; modern human beings do not struggle any more, but create a philosophy about God. In the
Old Testament the question is: 'Why have you, God of
my salvation, left me?' Today's question often is: 'If there
is a God, why is there so much suffering which cannot be
understood?' Third, in the Old Testament people essentially hold on to God in all their doubts, searching and
asking questions. Characteristic is the use of the possessive pronoun in many psalms of lament: 'Where are you,
my God?' In this way Job appeals to the God who hides,
to the God who lives and is his Redeemer (19:25).
Modern humans sometimes hardly know what prayer is;
they have discussions about God, whereas the Old
Testament believers cried out to God from their loss and
pain.

2.7 Breakthrough in God's hiding

Solid hope

Whoever calls upon God, as the authors of the psalms
do, will not be ashamed. In many passages of Scripture
the hiding of God leads to a breakthrough. That is why
we frequently read of the author of the psalm or the one
who prays that they hold on to the same God and hope,
even though they have the bitter and anxious experience
of God's absence. From the darkness and the questions
believers flee to God, who revealed himself as the faithful One who will not abandon the work of his hands.
They keep talking about 'my God', even with a lump in
their throat, so to speak. Even in the darkest psalm,
Psalm 88, the author calls the Lord 'the God who saves
me', though he is overwhelmed by distress. In the midst

of Job's despair he keeps trusting God and appeals 'from him to him': 'Even now my witness is in heaven; my advocate is on high. My intercessor is my friend as my eyes pour out tears to God; on behalf of a man he pleads with God...' (16:19-21). Full of restrained tension, Isaiah confesses: 'I will wait for the LORD, who is hiding his face from the house of Jacob. I will put my trust in him' (8:17). We read similar thoughts in Psalm 27:8-9, where in one and the same breath the author sighs: 'My heart says of you, Seek his face! Your face, LORD, I will seek. Do not hide your face from me, do not turn your servant away in anger; you have been my helper. Do not reject or forsake me, O God my Saviour.'

God's sovereign love and faithfulness

The most profound reason for God breaking through his hiding is not because of human beings and their searching and waiting upon him, but because of God himself, who goes his own way in sovereign freedom (cf. Ps. 77:19). Even in silence and in absence God does not forget those who belong to him. The silence is a breathing space in the conversation that God will continue. Israel's history is a living proof of it. Even the silent periods, the gaps, are used by God. How often people have to state, when they look back as Job did: 'Surely I spoke of things I did not understand, things too wonderful for me to know' (42:3).

There are many moments in the Old Testament which testify to the miraculous changing of God, when he comes from the darkness into the light and lets go of his anger. This change derives from God's faithful, incomprehensible love alone. This is what we read in the passage above, Deuteronomy 32, when God's judgement

is finally turned against the nations who rise against him
in mockery and want to destroy Israel. Moses' song finishes like this: 'Rejoice, O nations, with his people, for he
will avenge the blood of his servants; he will take
vengeance on his enemies and make atonement for his
land and people' (v. 43). In the same way the final words
of Ezekiel 39 are striking. In verses 23-24 God hiding his
face is explained as judgement on Israel's sin: '...the people of Israel went into exile for their sin, because they
were unfaithful to me. So I hid my face from them...'
Then there is a miraculous change in verse 25 which is
not motivated: 'Therefore this is what the Sovereign
LORD says: I will now bring Jacob back from captivity
and will have compassion on all the people of Israel, and
I will be zealous for my holy name.' The final words of
the prophecy are: 'I will no longer hide my face from
them, for I will pour out my Spirit on the house of Israel,
declares the Sovereign LORD' (v. 29).

The New Testament

In all of this there is a profound mystery which refers to
the One who lived through all our questions and anxi-
eties to the bottom, even more than we are ever able to
do. In the darkness of Golgotha the Son loudly cried out
to the Father: *'Eloi, Eloi, lama sabachthani?'* – which
means, 'My God, my God, why have you forsaken me?'
(Mt. 27:46). In these words from Psalm 22 the Lord Jesus
Christ made all our why's his own. In Christ being left
alone by God on the cross it is revealed what God really
intends: his holy love for people who already hid themselves from him in Paradise. Jesus was left alone so that
we will never be left alone. Whoever makes this his
refuge through faith knows, together with the author of
Psalm 9: 'Those who know your name will trust in you,

for you, LORD, have never forsaken those who seek you' (v. 10).

Questions

1. What does it mean for the practice of believing and waiting upon God that he has made himself known in an absolutely trustworthy way, but does not totally give himself in his revelation?

2. What do you think of the modern expression *Gottesfinsternis* ('the obscuration of God')?

3. Is it possible for Christians to recognize ithemselves in Psalm 88?

4. Is there a possible connection between the current spiritual and moral crisis in western societies, and a hiding of God?

5. Which way does the Bible show us to go on, even in times of spiritual emptiness and desolation?

Bibliography

Balentine, S.E., *The Hidden God. The Hiding of the Face of God in the Old Testament*, Oxford 1983.

Briend, J., *Dieu dans l'Écriture*, Paris 1992.

Hugger, P., *Jahwe meine Zuflucht*, Münster 1971.

Oosterhoff, B.J., *De afwezigheid Gods in het Oude Testament* (Apeldoornse Studies 1), Apeldoorn 1971.

Peels, H.G.L., *De omkeer van God in het Oude Testament* (Apeldoornse Studies 33), Apeldoorn 1997.

Perlitt, L., 'Die Verborgenheit Gottes', in: H.W. Wolff (Hsgb.), *Probleme biblischer Theologie* (Festschrift G. von Rad), München 1971, 367-382.

Reindl, J., *Das Angesicht Gottes im Sprachgebrauch des Alten Testaments* (ETS 25), Leipzig 1970.

Schrade, H., *Der verborgene Gott. Gottesbild und Gottesvorstellung in Israel und im alten Orient*, Stuttgart 1949.

Terrien, S., *The Elusive Presence. The Heart of Biblical Theology*, San Francisco 1978.

The Jealousy of God in the Old Testament

3.1 Problematic language

Jealousy as a human vice

Zeal, envy and jealousy are three concepts or terms which, in their modern usage, are closely related. In dictionaries the following meaning is given: zeal is 'a strong impulse or drive (to fulfil a task), a strong feeling (for something), active love (for an idea or a principle)'. Synonyms of zeal are enthusiasm and passion. Zeal can be positive or negative. There is 'holy' zeal, but also 'blind' zeal. Predominantly negative are the two other words, 'envy' and 'jealousy'. Of these two jealousy often gets the specific meaning of rivalry in love, jealousy connected with love and marriage. This jealousy is generally considered a human vice. We instinctively associate jealousy with petty-mindedness and greed, intolerance and egoism. Envious or jealous people begrudge things to other people, they cannot enjoy others' prosperity and happiness. From a psychological point of view, jealousy is one of the deepest, yet also one of the worst of human drives.

Jealous gods in Greece and Canaan

It is not surprising that, since humans are so frequently and fiercely controlled by jealousy, the gods in the myths and sagas of other nations are often envious or jealous as well. Greek mythology contains various tales in which the wife of the supreme god Zeus regularly plays the role of the jealous spouse. Thus Hera, queen of heaven and tutelary goddess of marriage, has every reason to treat her husband Zeus with suspicion. Zeus's excursions and adventures with other goddesses and mortal women are numerous.

Homer's famous epic about the Trojan war begins with the story of a wedding at which all the Olympian gods are present. All, that is, but one: Eris, the goddess of strife, is absent. Once the feast is in full swing, however, Eris suddenly enters the hall and throws into it a golden apple bearing the inscription 'For the most beautiful one'. Many female guests secretly hope they will possess the apple, but they forget about it when the goddesses Hera, Pallas Athena and Aphrodite claim the gift. Zeus, the supreme god, does not dare to cut this knot and refers the issue to Paris, the son of the king of Troy, who shall be the judge. The goddess of love, Aphrodite, is awarded the golden apple. Paris then discovers that he has aroused the wrath of the immensely jealous goddesses Hera and Pallas Athena. The battle for Troy and its destruction are the result.

In the world surrounding Israel in the times of the Old Testament, there was a strong awareness of the phenomenon of envy among the gods, and of jealous deities too. In Ugarit, a city in Northern Syria which was excavated from 1929 onwards, numerous texts have been found which shed light on our image of the religious world in which Israel lived after its entry into Canaan.

Particularly famous is the great Baal-cycle in which the death and resurrection of the rain and fertility god Baal is recounted. Of importance to us at this point is the text carrying the legend of Aqhat. This legend tells of Daniel, king of Ugarit, who grieves bitterly over the fact that he has no son. However, upon the intercession of Baal, the supreme god El blesses him with an heir whom he calls Aqhat. Daniel is proud of his son and gives him a miraculous bow, with which Aqhat is very successful in hunting. This arouses the envy of Anath, who is the goddess of both love and the hunt. She makes all sorts of promises to Aqhat, but he refuses to part with his bow and he is even rude to the goddess, which is a serious mistake. Following the encounter the jealous Anath has him eliminated by one of her warriors whom she has changed into an eagle. The consequences of Aqhat's death are striking: vegetation shrivels and for eight years there is no rain.

It will be clear that this kind of story about gods can only thrive in the context of polytheism. In many respects the gods and their mutual relations are a projection or an enlargement of what is found among human beings. On earth there is adultery, envy and jealousy; in the same way, the gods must have their vices and problems with the ways they relate to each other.

'Jealousy' or 'envy' of God in the Old Testament?

The average Bible reader, who understands and defines the concept of jealousy or envy along the above-mentioned lines, will encounter the notion of the jealousy or envy of God in many places throughout the Old Testament. They will experience this phenomenon as problematic and wonder how to deal with the 'shadow side' of God's self-revelation in the Old Testament. How is it possible that the eternal and truthful God, the Lord, is said to be jealous or envious? How can people whole-heartedly entrust themselves to a God whose 'envy' sometimes results in judgement and devastation? When we reflect upon these questions it is necessary to gain some insight into the biblical vocabulary. It is of great importance always to understand the key words of Scripture within their own context, with the timbre they have in Scripture itself, and to beware of the tendency to read our modern values into these biblcal words. When two people or texts say the same thing, it does not necessarily *mean* the same thing after all.

3.2 A short linguistic inquiry

The Hebrew word qin'ah

We start with a brief linguistic study. The word under review is the Hebrew word *qin'ah*. Hebrew has one word for the three words mentioned above: zeal, envy and jealousy. In each case we must determine from the context which nuance is relevant. The translation may vary as well. *Qin'ah* as 'zeal' may sometimes be translated as 'commitment, passion, ardour, energy, fierce emotion'; *qin'ah* as 'envy' may sometimes be translated as 'jealousy, grudging, rivalry, belligerence, competition'; *qin'ah* as 'jealousy' may sometimes be rendered 'suspicion, distrust'. In the Old Testament the word *qin'ah* (with its derivatives) occurs 85 times and proves to be applicable to various areas: marriage, economics, politics, religion. Still, for all the variation in usage, there is a common underlying notion, because in all the texts the reference is to an intense, energetic and vehement emotion which urges to action and results in actions.

Human and divine qin'ah

Upon closer scrutiny, however, there proves to be a fundamental difference between human *qin'ah* and divine *qin'ah*. It is striking that some of the difference is also reflected in the grammar. If the reference is to a negative, envious or jealous kind of zeal in the human sphere, *qin'ah* is construed with the Hebrew preposition b^e. But if the reference is to God's envy or jealousy, this preposition b^e (which indicates a negative intention) is never used. Instead we consistently encounter the preposition l^e.

3.3 Human *qin'ah*

Human zeal

In the Old Testament, human qin'ah can assume three forms: zeal, envy, or jealousy. We will briefly offer an example of each of these.

(i) Human zeal can be either negative or positive. What Edom felt against Israel was a negative zeal, says the prophet Ezekiel (35:11). What is going on here is not jealousy, but negative passion, a belligerent zeal, the will to exterminate the other. Joshua, who asks Moses to forbid Eldad and Medad to prophesy (Num. 11:28), exhibits a positive zeal. So does Phinehas, who, following Israel's idolatry with Baal-Peor, takes ardent action on behalf of God (Num. 25:11,13).

(ii) Human envy, it goes without saying, is negative. A graphic example of this is Rachel in Genesis 30, who

is envious of her sister Leah. This envy is resentment
at the prosperity of the other (the non-favourite wife
having many sons), tied in with grief over her own
childlessness. Another example is a specific theme in
the Psalms and Proverbs: envy at the prosperity of
the wicked, while the God-fearing person pines away
(e.g. Ps. 73:2-4).

(iii) Finally there is human jealousy in the context of marriage. Included in Numbers 5 is a special law with
reference to conjugal jealousy. There is mention here
of a 'spirit of jealousy' which comes over the husband in connection with the possible adultery of his
wife (v. 14). It is important to know that, except for
this verse in Numbers 5 and one other text in
Proverbs (6:34), this human *qin'ah* nowhere else
relates to conjugal jealousy.

It is precisely in connection with this last use of *qin'ah*,
however, that many authors interpret the meaning of
the *qin'ah* of God. An example occurs in Harry M.
Kuitert's *Signals from the Bible*: 'The ordinary – as distinguished from the specifically religious – language of
people can point the way. Numbers 5 tells us in what
sort of situation the word is most at home – the marriage
covenant ... To be jealous ... is not to brook any rivals.'
That is also how it is with God, who in making a
covenant has, as it were, established a marriage with
Israel: he does not tolerate rivals. 'Put it this way: we
can measure his faithfulness to his covenant by the
intensity of his jealousy. Were he a less passionate
husband, his jealousy would not be so keen.' Thus
Kuitert (and others) fill the notion of God's qin'ah very
emphatically with the idea of conjugal jealousy. But is
this correct? We shall see.

3.4 God is essentially 'the Jealous One'

God's self-revelation at Sinai

That God's jealousy is not something incidental or marginal but at the very centre of his self-revelation in the Old Testament is evident from a number of pivotal Scripture passages in which YHWH is directly characterized as 'the Jealous One'. The *qin'ah* of God is not an emotion, a mood, but something that is integral to his being. Furthermore, in this context all thoughts of egoism, fear of losing his possession, envy or resentment are lacking.

The core texts are Exodus 34 and the Ten Commandments in Exodus 20 (or Deuteronomy 5), where God reveals himself in an act of covenant-making. Exodus 34 follows the story of the golden calf (Ex. 32). After Moses' intercession God forgives this breach of covenant and Israel receives the covenant charter, the two tablets of stone, once more. Then the Lord proceeds to teach the people the essence of the covenant. Israel is not allowed to make a covenant with the Canaanites (Ex. 34:12), for on such occasions the names of foreign gods would be invoked and the danger of idolatry would become very real. Verse 14 reads: 'Do not worship any other god, for the LORD, whose name is Jealous, is a jealous God.' God's name is *qanna'*, and the name denotes his being. God's covenant with Israel is based on the legitimate claim that God has on Israel. He loves this people; he has delivered them from bondage; he has led them out of the house of bondage; and when he calls himself *qanna'*, it has to do with his intense reaction to the violation of his rights and the breach of covenant that has occurred (ch. 32). He is the God of Israel: that excludes others. Israel's worship is their privilege. It is not the image of a jealous husband which dominates this passage, but that of the Ruler who in his treaty with his vassal tolerates no other Lord except himself and defends his claims upon his subjects.

The same is true in the Ten Commandments, where the prohibition of any graven image or any likeness is motivated by the words: 'for I, the LORD your God, am a jealous God...' The   second commandment primarily means that people are not allowed to make an image of God in order to worship him that way. The incomparable God cannot, by means of a material representation, be put on a level with idols. So when it is said that he is a jealous God, it means that he watches over his rights and stands by his holiness. This divine zeal has two aspects: he is a jealous God who on the one hand visits the iniquity of the fathers upon the children, and on the other hand shows steadfast love to thousands of those who love him. Here we see how clearly God's jealousy functions within the special relationship he has with Israel, where it can mean either a blessing or a curse, either life or death, for those who keep the covenant or violate it.

Some core texts from Deuteronomy and Joshua

Let us briefly touch on a couple of other core texts in which the Lord is directly called 'the jealous God'. Deuteronomy 4 is completely on the same wavelength as the second commandment. Moses brings home to the people that they must not forget the covenant with God by making graven images (v. 23), 'for the LORD your God is a consuming fire, a jealous God' (v. 24). Typical here is the allusion to the event on Mount Sinai when God spoke from the midst of the fire (vv. 12,15,23,36).

In combination with the first commandment the Lord is called 'a jealous God' in Deuteronomy 6:14-15: 'Do not follow other gods, the gods of the peoples around you; for the LORD your God, who is among you, is a jealous God and his anger will burn against you, and he will destroy you from the face of the land.' In Deuteronomy 6:4 we have the famous *shema'*, Israel's basic creed: 'Hear, O Israel: The LORD our God, the LORD is one.' God being one and singular for Israel, Israel must also be one and undivided before the Lord (v. 5: 'with all your heart and with all your soul and with all your strength'). Serving other gods means a breach in the covenant of love and faithfulness. It prompts God to be zealous in his jealousy.

Similarly connected with the establishment of the covenant on Mount Sinai and with the first commandment is Joshua 24. The people of Israel have said: 'Far be it from us to forsake the LORD to serve other gods!' (v. 16). But Joshua said to the people: 'You are not able to serve the LORD. He is a holy God; he is a jealous God. He will not forgive your rebellion and your sins. If you forsake the LORD and serve foreign gods, he will turn and bring disaster on you and make an end of you, after he has been good to you' (vv. 19-20). The reverse side of belonging to the Lord is renouncing foreign gods. Joshua here underscores the seriousness of serving God by referring to his jealousy at the same time as his holiness and on the same level with it.

In all these passages the Lord reveals himself to his people as a God who will not be mocked, who does not just let things take their course, and who is not indifferent to how people deal with his word, his laws, and his covenant. He is serious when he says that he loves his people, and contempt of that love angers him. He is the living God who reacts with powerful intensity. It is a reaction rooted in his zeal and jealousy.

3.5 The operation of God's *qin'ah*

Against Israel and related to idolatry

In a great many passages we find a description or prophecy of how God's jealousy is aroused to action. The words that were spoken at the time of the establishment of the covenant were in all seriousness incarnated in reality. First of all, Israel itself has to deal with God's jealousy when it lapses into idolatry. Especially striking and expressive on this point is the song of Moses in Deuteronomy 32. God threatens Israel with judgement, the judgement of his self-concealment. Why? 'They made me jealous by what is no god and angered me with their worthless idols. I will make them envious by those who are not a people; I will make them angry by a nation that has no understanding' (v. 21). The same warning came through in verses 16-17, a text which is cited by Paul in the New Testament in connection with the Lord's Supper (clinging to old forms of idolatry besides being a Christian could provoke God to jealousy; Christians need to choose between the table of the Lord and the table of demons, 1 Cor. 10:21-22). The song of Moses describes the very intimate relationship between God and Israel. As a result of the covenant between them, God and his people form a sort of 'circle'. That which lies outside that circle is called 'no god' and 'no people'. But now Israel provokes God to jealousy by giving preference to those foreign gods, those 'non-gods'. This provokes God's wrath and his holy will to maintain his claims, to tolerate no such infringement of his honour. This is his 'jealousy' which brings judgement upon Israel.

In particular the prophet Ezekiel speaks frequently of God's jealousy. Most trenchant is his message in

Chapters 16 and 23, in which he depicts the relation between Israel and the Lord as a marriage relationship in which the bride (Jerusalem) becomes even worse than a prostitute, a bride who runs after her lovers, the idol gods. God's reaction is stated in 16:38: 'I will sentence you to the punishment of women who commit adultery and who shed blood; I will bring upon you the blood vengeance of my wrath and jealous anger' (cf. 16:42 and 23:25). God's *qin'ah* here is that of an enraged, offended husband. Prominent, however, is not God's jealousy but his anger, for his *qin'ah* is directed against an adulterous Israel, not against his rivals, the competing gods.

Against the nations for what they did to Israel

God's jealousy, however, can also turn against the nations when they lay violent hands on his covenant people. An example of this is Ezekiel 36, a prophecy 'to the mountains', i.e. to Israel. The enemy scoffs and shows off (v. 2). 'This is what the Sovereign LORD says: in my burning zeal I have spoken against the rest of the nations, and against Edom, for with glee and with malice in their hearts they made my land their own possession so that they might plunder its pasture-land' (v. 5). The Lord is here reacting to the violation of his rights. They have plundered Israel, i.e. 'my land' (v. 5). God's jealousy will not just let this happen.

Exactly the same message is heard in the opening words of the prophecy of Nahum against wicked Nineveh which oppresses the world: 'The LORD is a jealous and avenging God; the LORD takes vengeance and is filled with wrath. The LORD takes vengeance on his foes and maintains his wrath against his enemies' (Nah. 1:2). Clearly, there is no suggestion of jealousy. The reference is to God's angry but saving intervention; he does not let his honour be violated, but punishes the enemy.

For Israel in relation to God's plan of salvation

Certain passages also speak very positively about God's jealousy as his saving intervention on behalf of Israel. Most expressive is Isaiah 9, the beloved prophecy about the people who now walk in darkness but will see a great light. Isaiah must have held his breath when he came to the heart of his prophecy: 'For to us a child is born, to us a son is given, and the government will be on his shoulders. And he will be called Wonderful Counsellor, Mighty God, Everlasting Father, Prince of Peace' (v. 6). By way of this child the Lord gives a new future to his people, who threaten to sink away into darkness for ever. Then, in verse 7, the prophecy ends with the words: 'The zeal of the LORD Almighty will accomplish this.' It is God's *qin'ah* which is the driving force behind this decisive turn in the history of salvation. His burning love and fiery drive, his zeal, are behind the night of Christmas, behind Golgotha, Easter morning and Pentecost. He does not forsake the work of his hands. In his zeal he completes the realization of his plan of redemption.

3.6 Conclusions

God's qin'ah: jealousy or watching over privileges?

By way of a summary we draw three conclusions. In the first place we observe that in the Old Testament there is a clear difference between the human and the divine *qin'ah*. God's *qin'ah* never denotes mere envy. Human envy or jealousy can be completely misguided or assume nasty forms, but God's *qin'ah* always has a cause, a reason and purpose. Although it sometimes comes with devastating effect, divine zeal always serves a positive end: the restoration of the covenant, the vindication of God's holiness. Human jealousy is something incidental; God's zeal is something essential. It is incorrect to define God's jealousy completely in terms of the image of conjugal jealousy, the word *qin'ah* is seldom used in relation to marriage. Furthermore, God's zeal is not directed, in jealousy, against threatening rivals, but, in wrath, against an adulterous Israel. God's zeal does not consist in malice or jealousy vis-à-vis foreign gods; instead it watches over his privileges and punishes their violation.

Biblical-theological setting

A second conclusion concerns the biblical-theological setting of the Old Testament references to the *qin'ah* of God. We mention three things:

(i) God's covenant. In the background of God's jealousy there is almost always the reality of the covenant. In his love and electing compassion he has bound himself to Israel. He is the Father, King and Shepherd of this people. When Israel violates the rules of the covenant, indeed even breaks the covenant (especially in the form of idolatry and image worship), the Lord, as it were, 'owes it to himself' to react. This reaction, in all its energy and ardour, is God's *qin'ah*.

(ii) God's holiness. Some exegetes rightly portray the jealousy of God as the active side of his holiness (cf. Is. 42:13). A symbol of the destructive and purifying holiness of God (Ex. 3) is the burning fire with which God's jealousy is frequently compared. God's jealousy is the maintenance of God's honour and name in situations where his holiness is violated.

(iii) God's wrath. The majority of the passages in which the qin'ah of God is mentioned have the dark colour of wrath and judgement. In this context wrath is the instrument or expression of jealousy, while the jealousy itself refers to the deeper roots. Sometimes the words 'wrath' and 'jealousy' are virtually synonymous.

God's qin'ah *characterizes his revelation*

Finally we can state that God's jealousy is characteristic of his self-revelation in the Old Testament. In the world surrounding Israel there are numerous examples of jealous gods. They involve two things: either the attitude of the deity towards humans (in connection with their prosperity, or beautiful women, etc., or bad relations among the gods themselves). However, God's jealousy in the Old Testament pertains to the maintenance of his rights, in connection with which other gods simply vanish beyond the horizon. In fact, this sort of jealousy was something unique, even shocking, to the world of the Ancient Near East, where a fundamental religious tolerance prevailed. The temple of a specific deity frequently featured space where sacrifices could be made to another deity as well. This is very different from the Old Testament where the theme is: one people and one God whose name is *el qanna*. For above the tumult of gods and people stands the Lord who puts his hand upon his people, upon all his children, and says: 'You are mine.' 'I am the LORD; that is my name! I will not give my glory to another or my praise to idols' (Is. 42:8). The message of God's jealousy, accordingly, does not put God's Old Testament self-revelation in the shadows, but in full daylight.

Questions

1. What exactly does Paul mean when he says that he watches the church of Corinth 'with a godly jealousy' (2 Cor. 11:2, compare Num. 25:11)?

2. Why is Kuitert's attempt to fill out the notion of God's revenge with the idea of conjugal jealousy not really adequate?

3. What does the proclamation of God's jealousy tell us about God himself?

4. How would you react if, on Christmas Day, your minister is not preaching about Luke 2, but about the text from Isaiah 9:7: 'The *zeal* of the LORD Almighty will accomplish this'?

5. Try to define the difference between the way ancient mythology talks about the gods' jealousy and the way the Bible speaks of God's jealousy. Why is the difference so remarkable?

Bibliography

Bell, R.H., *Provoked to Jealousy. The Origin and Purpose of the Jealousy Motif in Rom. 9-11* (WUNT 63), Tübingen 1994.

Berg, W., 'Die Eifersucht Gottes – ein problematischer Zug des alttestamentlichen Gottesbildes?', *Biblische Zeitschrift* 23 (1979), 197-211.

Brongers, H.A., 'Der Eifer des Herrn Zebaoth', *Vetus Testamentum* 13 (1963), 269-284.

Dohmen, C., '"Eifersüchtiger ist sein Name" (Ex 34,14). Ursprung und Bedeutung der alttestamentlichen Rede von Gottes Eifersucht', *Theologisches Zeitschrift* 46 (1990), 289-304.

Kuitert, H.M., *Signals from the Bible*, Grand Rapids 1972 (translation of: De spelers en het spel, Amsterdam 1964).

Moor, J.C. de, *The Rise of Yahwism. The Roots of Israelite Monotheism*, Leuven 1990.

Peels, H.G.L., lemma qn', in: W.A. VanGemeren (ed.), *New International Dictionary of Old Testament Theology and Exegesis* Volume III, Carlisle 1997, 937-940.

von Rad, G., *Theologie des Alten Testaments. Band I: Die Theologie der geschichtlichen* Überlieferungen Israels, München 1987.

Renaud, B., *Je suis un Dieu jaloux. Evolution sémantique et signification théologique de qine'ah*, Paris 1963.

The Repentance of God in the Old Testament

4.1 A problem for faith and theology

Repentance because of failure

The Old Testament references to the repentance of God are confusing to many Bible readers. 'Repentance', after all, implies the notions of grief and regret over something one has done wrong and desires to amend. Repentance means regret over something of which one later says: it was wrong, foolish, or sinful. 'If I had considered it more carefully, I would not have said or done it that way.' In the background of repentance there is sinful stubbornness or culpable ignorance. That is the case with human repentance in the Old Testament (Job 42:6; Jer. 8:6; 31:19; Ex. 13:17).

Contradictions in Scripture?

It is remarkable that this human repentance is mentioned only four times. All the other texts (more than 35) in which the Hebrew root with the meaning 'to repent' (*nchm* niphal) occurs refer to the repentance of God. It is no wonder that the theme of divine repentance poses problems to people. Is the idea of a God who goes back on his deeds or words not unbiblical? Does the Bible itself not say that in God there is no change or shadow due to change (Jas. 1:17)? Does the Bible contradict itself on this point? Besides, does the idea of a God who repents not push people into fear and uncertainty? Can God ever say: 'Sorry, I did something wrong', or 'If only I had known this in advance'? Is a God who can be sorry not fundamentally unpredictable and capricious?

Undervaluation and overvaluation

Many theologians have, of course, reflected on these questions. The result has been that they have taken two totally different directions on this issue. On the one hand, particularly in the early centuries, one can observe a strong tendency to undervalue this biblical reference to God's repentance. Greek versions of the Old Testament (e.g. the Septuagint) sometimes fail to translate the notion of God's repentance accurately at all, and use verbs such as 'being gracious' or 'being angry' in the place of the verb 'repent' which occurs in the Hebrew Bible. The Jewish-Alexandrian scholar Philo, a contemporary of Jesus, stated that it is the height of wickedness to say that God has emotional attributes. The defective language of Scripture is the result of God's accommodating himself to us humans. God is like a physician who sometimes uses deceptive language in order to heal people. To Philo God is the highest kind of being, the immutable, impassive, unmoved Mover. Many scholars, following him, considered texts about God's repentance as improper figurative speech, having no real revelational value.

Alongside this undervaluation, but to a significantly lesser degree, there is also in history an overvaluation of the biblical references to God's repentance. Scholars sometimes appealed to Genesis 1:26-27 and said that if humans are created in the image of God, then God himself must also be somewhat anthropomorphic. These ideas have been advanced by the Dutch theologian Harry Kuitert (amongst others), who asserts that God is entirely as he is in his revelation to humankind, and enters into a relationship with them. There is no longer any residual something 'behind' this revelation. God's essence lies in his covenantal drive towards partnership. The way the Bible speaks about God's repentance, says Kuitert, must liberate us from all the problems inherent in speaking about his immutability. God can even repent of his non-repentance and follow up on his last word with an ultimate word, the word of grace. In my opinion, the way in which the Bible speaks about God's repentance is overvalued here. Let us open the Old Testament itself.

Two categories

The relevant texts can be divided into two categories. On the one hand, there are texts which speak of God's repentance 'for evil'. By this expression we mean the repentance of God which results in misfortune, in judgement, for humans. In addition there are texts which speak of God's repentance 'for good'. By this expression we mean the grief which God feels over a threatened or already executed judgement, with the result that this judgement is terminated or not yet carried out. It is striking that in the majority of the texts God's repentance is 'for good'. In only two cases is God's repentance 'for evil': in the history of the flood (Gen. 6) and in the rejection of Saul (1 Sam. 15).

4.2 God's repentance 'for evil'

Before or after the flood

Immediately, at the outset of human history, things had already got to the point where the repentance of God had to be broached. 'The LORD saw ... that every inclination of the thoughts of his heart was only evil all the time' (Gen. 6:5). The whole earth was corrupt (v. 12). Titanism, rebellion, and tyranny prevailed everywhere (6:1-4). We read on: 'The LORD was grieved [sorry, RSV] that he had made man on the earth, and his heart was filled with pain' (v. 6). The use of the word 'grief' in the text is significant. God is deeply touched. He is not unmoved: judgement is connected with grief. What does it mean, in this passage, that God is sorry, that he 'repents'? It does not mean that God is sorry over something he would not have done had he known in advance how things would turn out. God's 'repentance' is that he looks, with much distaste and pain, at how things are going with humankind and that he changes his conduct with respect to humankind.

That God's repentance does not flow from a sense of having acted wrongly is evident from what follows. The creation of humankind was not wrong in itself. Even when judgement comes, God definitely still holds on to humankind. After verse 7 comes verse 8 with grace for Noah. And at the end of this story there is 8:21, where God says: 'Never again will I curse the ground because of man, even though every inclination of his heart is evil from childhood. And never again will I destroy all living creatures, as I have done.' Humans are unchanged and unchangeably evil, but God moves on. He holds on to his original intent – by another route to the same goal.

Interesting and revealing is a comparison of Genesis Chapters 6-9 with Babylonian flood stories as we know them from the Gilgamesh epic (in the Atrachasis epic there is an almost identical story). In the eleventh tablet of the Gilgamesh epic we are told how, for a number of vague reasons, the gods have decided to destroy humankind by means of a flood. But the god Ea passed on this decision, by way of a reed partition, to a certain Utnapishtim with the advice to go and build a ship. On this ship Utnapishtim, along with his family and many animals, survives. After the flood Utnapishtim brings an offering to the gods. In this context we are told that the gods come upon the odour of the offering like flies, because for such a long time they have been deprived of offerings. The gods 'repent', deeply regretting that they released the flood upon the earth.

Comparing this story to that in Genesis 6-9, we immediately sense a clear difference. In the Gilgamesh epic the 'repentance' of the gods is grief over their own short-sightedness and incomprehension. Their grief concerns their own conduct, their own wrongheaded decisions. In the Bible, however, God's repentance is not caused by belated insight into his own mistaken conduct, but it is precisely the motive of the flood. Because God is God, he needs to react to the evil done by humankind. In short, the repentance of the gods in the Gilgamesh epic is a human kind of repentance, whereas the repentance of God in Genesis 6-9 is divine.

Repentance over Saul

The second passage is 1 Samuel 15. Saul has failed to fully execute the ban on Amalek. God responds by saying: 'I am grieved [RSV: I repent] that I have made Saul king, because he has turned away from me and has not carried out my instructions' (v. 11). Also the conclusion of this chapter (v. 35) reports God's 'repentance' over

Saul's kingship. God is sorry, not because he has done something wrong, but because Saul has. God's 'repentance' marks the end of his elective dealing with Israel through Saul. At the same time God does not take back his decision to let Israel have a king (1 Sam. 8:7,9,22). In 15:28 Saul is told that Israel's kingdom will not be suspended but given to another, a better king – David.

When we compare Genesis 6 with 1 Samuel 15 we discover that in both places God's repentance means a change in his conduct; he is partially going back on what he did before in order to be able to continue the project all the better. In Genesis 8 this is a renewed and purified beginning with humankind; in 1 Samuel 15 it is a 'better' king. In both passages the repentance of God is prompted by the sin and unfaithfulness of humans.

'For he is not a man...'

In the same chapter (1 Sam. 15), between the words about God's repentance in verse 11 and verse 36, there is a text in which we are told that God does not repent. Verse 29 reads: 'He who is the Glory of Israel does not lie or change his mind [RSV: repent], for he is not a man, that he should change his mind [RSV: repent].' How can these two things possibly occur in the same chapter? From the context it is evident that Saul gave a rather lame excuse along the lines of 'let bygones be bygones' (vv. 24-25). Saul has little notion of the holiness of God and humanizes him. He wants a quick and painless settlement. But that God is serious about his word of judgement (that another man will be made king of Israel) is brought home in verse 29. God refuses to be mollified. He is not going to change his mind. God is not like a human – superficial, unstable, talking one way one moment and another way at another time.

Thus the talk about God's 'repentance' in 1 Samuel 15 has two aspects, both of which are true and which complement (rather than correct) each other: on the one hand, that God 'repents' having made Saul king (vv. 11,36), but this does not mean caprice or uncertainty (v. 29); on the other, that God is not a human who lies and goes back on his word (v. 29), but this does not mean that God cannot react or modify his conduct (vv. 11,36). In summary: God's repentance is a reality, a reaction to human misconduct, but, unlike human repentance, it is not fickle or arbitrary.

Precisely the same idea occurs in Numbers 23:19 in the midst of the story of Balaam. Balak cajoles Balaam into going with him from one vantage point to another in the hope that this malediction expert will be sure not to bless but to curse Israel down below in the valley. This would indeed be worth trying with the servant of any deity whatever, but the God who prompts Balaam to speak is different. 'God is not a man, that he should lie, nor a son of man, that he should change his mind. Does he speak and then not act? Does he promise and not fulfil?' (v. 19). 'You must not think, Balak,' says Balaam, 'that the God who makes me pronounce a blessing upon Israel will later change his mind and go back on this action. He is God and not a human being.' This statement, too, does not mean that God cannot 'repent', but it does mean that God does not 'repent' in human fashion.

4.3 God's repentance 'for good'

Stopping a judgement in progress

As stated above, the Old Testament message of God's repentance for the most part ends with benefits for humans. It is in their favour, 'for good'. This can mean that God cuts short or stops the judgement upon sin that is already well under way. An example of this is Jeremiah 42:10. In this chapter we find ourselves looking at the end of Judah's history. Jerusalem has been destroyed; numerous exiles have been taken to Babylon. Gedaliah, the governor appointed by Nebuchadnezzar, has been assassinated by Jewish patriots. Captain Johanan now wants to flee to Egypt with the Judeans who have survived, but first asks Jeremiah for the way God is pointing. The Lord's answer is surprising: 'If you stay in this land, I will build you up and not tear you down; I will plant you and not uproot you, for I am grieved over the disaster [RSV: repent of the evil] I have inflicted on you.' These words about building and planting, tearing down and rooting up, also occur in Jeremiah's call (Jer. 1:9-10). But now they occur in reverse! The time for building has come. At this turning point we hear of God's repentance. The 'evil' of which God is now repenting is the conquest of the land and the abduction of the people into exile. It is not at all that God thinks he was wrong in inflicting this catastrophe upon Judah, but he can no longer bear to see it happen. He stops the judgement, ends the period of uprooting, and wants to start planting again. God's repentance is the very last resort after the judgement has been initiated. (Also cf. 2 Sam. 24:16 and 1 Chr. 21:15)

Delay of an announced judgement

God's repentance 'for good' even more frequently implies that he does not, or does not yet, carry out the disasters he has announced. His repentance, is as it were, an act of self-control, of setting limits to his wrath. Two examples may clarify this.

We find the first example in the visions of Amos, where God again 'repents' after the intercession of the prophet. Amos has five visions, the first two of which end with God's repentance. The first vision shows the threatening disaster of a locust plague, but Amos cries out: 'Sovereign LORD, forgive! How can Jacob survive? He is so small!' (7:2). In reply the Lord repented (NIV, NRSV: 'relented') concerning this and said that it would not happen (7:3). In the second vision the prophet sees the looming misfortune by fire. Now he no longer begs for forgiveness but cries out: 'Sovereign LORD, I beg you, stop! How can Jacob survive? He is so small!' And again the Lord repents (vv. 5-6). But in the third vision God sets a limit, and Amos no longer prays. The time of God's repentance is over. Judgement is on its way (cf. Hos. 13:14; Jer. 4:28; 15:6; 20:16; Ezek. 24:14; Zech. 8:14). This passage in Amos clearly shows what God's repentance is. It is a deferment of judgement. Why? Because the plan of judgement was wrong? No. Note the fact that Amos prays: 'forgive', which implies the recognition of guilt.

The second text, Hosea 11, is the most moving. In it God opens up his heart in a generous way. 'When Israel was a child, I loved him' (v. 1). How God had cherished and cared for Israel! But they strayed from him. Therefore – you can absolutely count on it! – judgement is on its way (vv. 5-7). Then, in verse 8, an amazing shift occurs: 'How can I give you up, Ephraim? How can I hand you over, Israel? How can I treat you like Admah? How can I make you like Zeboiim? My heart is changed within me; all my compassion is aroused' [cf. KJV]. I cannot do it, God says; I cannot let Israel go down in judgement for ever, as happened with Admah and Zeboiim, cities near Sodom and Gomorrah which were overturned. And why can God not do this? Because in his own heart a reversal is taking place as a result of his 'repentance'. God's repentance brings about what Israel's vainly awaited repentance cannot bring about. He will not once and for all execute his fierce anger, for he is God and not a human, the Holy One in the midst of his people (v. 9). This does not mean, however, that judgement is totally out of the question, for the prophecy ends with the words that God will one day lead his people from Egypt and Assyria (places of exile to which, therefore, Israel will be taken) in order to settle them for good in safety (v. 11). God's repentance is an expression of his triumphant love, a love which sets limits to his wrath, because he will proceed and complete his plan of salvation.

4.4 God's repentance in Israel's confession

God's repentance and the two aspects of the covenant

The repentance of God in the Old Testament can even be articulated in a dogmatic fashion, as it were, and become a part of Israel's confession. God's repentance is a reality with which God's people have to deal daily. Telling in this respect is Jeremiah 18, where Jeremiah has to draw a lesson from the work of a potter. We will confine ourselves to citing verses 6b-10:

> Like clay in the hand of the potter, so are you in my hand, O house of Israel. If at any time I announce that a nation or kingdom is to be uprooted, torn down and destroyed, and if that nation I warned repents of its evil, then I will relent [RSV: repent of the evil] and not inflict on it the disaster I had planned. And if at another time I announce that a nation or kingdom is to be built up and planted, and if it does evil in my sight and does not obey me, then I will reconsider the good [RSV: repent of the good] I had intended to do for it.

Within the context of the message of God's repentance the two sides of the covenant, blessing and curse, are stated in one formula. The reference is to a fundamental feature in the conduct of God. God's word is not rigid and mechanical. He reacts; his repentance is directly oriented to the conduct of humans.

Pleading on the basis of God's repentance

To the Israelites, accordingly, it was not contradictory when the prophet Joel, in reciting the ancient confession known from Exodus 34 concerning the attributes of God, also mentioned the repentance of God in his summons to repentance: 'Return to the LORD your God, for he is gracious and compassionate, slow to anger and abounding in love, and he relents from sending calamity [RSV: and repents of evil]' (2:13b). The Lord loves to repent of the judgement he has threatened, to restrain and defer it. In that way God's repentance is a powerful source of hope, a ground on which to plead for mercy (cf. Jon. 4:2).

The divine 'perhaps'

Immediately after the confession in Joel 2:12-13 come the words: 'Who knows? He may turn and have pity and leave behind a blessing – grain offerings and drink offerings for the LORD your God' (v. 14). 'Who knows...?' These words recur elsewhere. It is the divine 'perhaps' (see also Jon. 3:9; Amos 5:15; and Zeph. 2:3). What does this 'perhaps' of divine repentance mean? It is not an expression of doubt but of living hope (see the preceding confession in Joel 2:13). Furthermore, this 'perhaps' is not based on uncertainty vis-à-vis the whims of an incalculable God, but arises from the humility of those who know they have no rights and who are completely dependent on divine grace (cf. Lam. 3:29). Ultimately this 'perhaps' highlights God's sovereign freedom, the freedom to act also with respect to his wrath.

4.5 God's repentance and the New Testament

God unrepentant

As frequently as God's repentance is mentioned in the Old Testament, so sporadically does it appear in the New. Actually the New Testament only says that God does not repent. God is 'the Father of the heavenly lights, who does not change like shifting shadows' (Jas. 1:17, cf. Rom. 11:29; Heb. 7:21; Heb. 6:18; Tit. 1:2).

Correction or salvation history

What is the reason why the theme of God's repentance is missing in the New Testament? We reject the opinion that in this regard the New Testament seeks to purge itself of excessively anthropomorphic ideas about God. That, of course, would mean a split between the Old and the New Testament revelation of God. It is much more likely that we must search for a reason in the progress of the history of redemption. In the Old Testament God's repentance always has to do with his judgement. In the coming of Jesus Christ, however, God's work of salvation has reached both its nadir and its zenith. God's judgement upon sin is realized on the cross in the Only-Beloved. Everyone who is in Christ has peace with God. The wrath of God abides till the day of his final judgement on all those who reject the Son. In this field of tension between the 'already' and 'not yet' there is no room for the repentance of God, for judgement has come in Christ and will come on the last day.

4.6 Conclusions

Similarity and difference

We want to draw two conclusions. God's repentance is not the same as human repentance. There is indeed a certain similarity, namely that repentance carries with it a change in conduct and may be accompanied by intense emotions. But, most of all, there is a great difference: God's repentance never arises from a sense of having fallen short or from culpable ignorance. The rendering 'repentance', accordingly, has to be viewed as a makeshift translation. A variety of texts explicitly indicate that it is incorrect to put God's repentance on a level with human repentance (Num. 23; 1 Sam. 15; Hos. 11). The two 'sequences' of God's repentance and God's unrepentance are by no means contradictory, but instead complement each other. The sequences about God's repentance indicate that the Lord is a living God who can react to real humans, and who is not a static abstraction. The sequences about God's unrepentance indicate that his repentance does not imply arbitrariness and that in all things, regardless of circumstances, God's plan of redemption continues undiminished.

With a somewhat halting analogy, one may think of two terms from the art of war: strategy and tactics. The strategy is the overall plan, covering everything from the phase of preparation up to and including the description of military objectives. Tactics encompass the entire range of military operations, which are aimed at the realization of the strategy. During any given military engagement the tactics may change many times, while a good military commander nevertheless keeps a firm grip on his strategy. This is how one could picture the Old Testament notion of the repentance of God: it concerns

his actions on the level of tactics (God 'repents'), while
the overall strategic plan remains firmly fixed (God cannot 'repent').

The living God

The message concerning God's repentance is most significant. In fact, it is not a 'dark' side of the Old
Testament revelation of God, but constitutes a ray of
light into it, which shows clearly that all abstraction or
spiritualization of the image we have of the Lord God is
impossible, because God is the Living One. He is not the
Unmoved Mover of Philo, or a computer-God of ice-
crystal. Nor is he the all-too-human Partner-God of
Kuitert. He is the deeply empathetic Lord who, in his
vital contact with this world, and especially with his
people, goes his own way, not statically but reactively
and closely, while all the time he remains the same in his
holiness and love.

Questions

1. Have you ever met other people who had problems
   with the way the Old Testament speaks about God's
   repentance? How did you react to what they said?

2. In the biblical story of the flood God's repentance
   comes at the beginning. In the Babylonian story, the
   gods' repentance comes at the end. What do you
   think is the meaning of this?

3. After our survey of the meaning of God's repentance,
   what can be said generally about the use of human
   concepts in describing God's way of acting?

4. Do you know a better translation of the Hebrew word *nchm*, which is usually translated as 'repentance', in its application to God's acts?

5. How can we use the biblical speech of God's repentance in knowing God and relating to him?

Bibliography

Brueggemann, W., *Theology of the Old Testament. Testimony, Dispute, Advocacy*, Minneapolis 1997.

Fretheim, T., 'The Repentance of God: A Key to Evaluating Old Testament God-talk', *Horizons in Biblical Theology* 10 (1988), 47-70.

Jeremias, J., *Die Reue Gottes. Aspekte alttestamentlicher Gottesvorstellung*, Neukirchen-Vluyn 1975.

Kaiser, O., *Der Gott des Alten Testaments. Theologie des AT 1: Grundlegung*, Göttingen 1993.

Kuitert, H.M., *De mensvormigheid Gods. Een dogmatisch-hermeneuti-sche studie over de anthropomorfismen van de Heilige Schrift*, Kampen 1962.

Kuyper, L.J., 'The Suffering and Repentance of God', *Scottish Journal of Theology* 22 (1969), 257-277.

Michaeli, F., *Dieu à l'image de l'homme. Etude de la notion anthropomorfique de Dieu dans l'Ancien Testament*, Neuchâtel 1950.

Smith, R.L., *Old Testament Theology. Its History, Method, and Message*, Nashville 1993.

5

The Vengeance of God in the Old Testament

5.1 Introduction: annoyance and offence

The image of God blurred and humanized

Whoever speaks about the 'God of revenge' certainly meets misunderstanding, annoyance and even pity in his immediate environment. It is perhaps more difficult for contemporary humans than it has ever been in the history of humankind. In the climate of modern religion in which we live, there is very little room for the idea of a God who inflicts retribution or punishment, not to mention the idea of a God who executes vengeance. Periodic inquiries into the situation of religion and church-relatedness show a progressive blurring of faith in a personal God. For most people God is more a 'something' than a 'Someone.' There is an ever-deepening sense of uncertainty with respect to the big question: actually and truly, who is God? It is easy to understand that if the personhood of God has already become extremely problematic for many people, this is certainly the case with Old Testament discourse about God as king, warrior, judge and avenger. As we look around us, we see in our society the generally increasing humanization and levelling of the image of God. In this connection, all the emphasis falls on the love, pity, or even powerlessness of God. Increasingly people tend to filter out of their image of God notions such as wrath, punishment and judgement. That's something I can no longer buy, says the modern theologian. I can't picture that, says the person in the street.

Offence for the Bible reader

But the faithful Bible reader has definite problems in this area as well. How can the Bible possibly speak of the 'vengeance' of God? Does this not border on blasphemy? How can one possibly speak about God with a term that has such negative associations? In serious conversation with our children about having a quarrel with other children, we teach them that they may not exchange tit for tat. But if we subsequently read in the Bible that God avenges himself, we have a problem. How can I explain this to my children? In current usage vengeance suggests action that is high-handed, illegitimate, and immoral. It is something not done. We intuitively associate vengeance with hatred, vindictiveness and cruelty. Vengeance is incompatible with justice. A German proverb reads: 'Revenge turns a droplet of justice into a flood of injustice.' And a Flemish saying is: 'Revenge is honey in the mouth but poison in the heart.'

God and the Greek gods of vengeance

Ancient Greek mythology knew deities whose speciality was vengeance – especially female deities who were called the Furies. Most famous among them was Megaera, a frightening being depicted with snakes, whips and torches, whose speciality it was to avenge the murder of family members. It was her job to pursue

criminals and drive them insane. Whoever reads the
Bible with this sort of story in mind will certainly ask
questions. How should we understand the biblical picture of the God of vengeance? Especially urgent is the
question of whether this God is indeed the same as him
upon whom we call with childlike reverence as our
Father in heaven, a God who graciously forgives.

It is the Bible itself which gives us a decisive answer.
It is immensely important, therefore, that in reading the
Bible we learn to know well the language of the Bible,
the biblical ABC. Sometimes key words in Scripture have
such a deep meaning that they say far more than the
same words do in our own language. For example, the
Hebrew words *'ahabah* ('love') or *'èmèt* ('truth') are much
richer in content than the corresponding words in our
language. The same is true of the Hebrew root nqm,
'vengeance/to avenge'. Whereas in our use of this word
it is very negative in character, a word that is the
antonym of justice, the Hebrew nqm virtually always
has an eminently positive meaning. In the Old Testament
vengeance is a means of restoring justice, of redressing a
wrong. Vengeance is not opposed to justice, but is exer-
cised in the service of justice. This is also evident in four
core texts in which God's vengeance is mentioned. I call
them core texts or key texts because they occur at pivotal
places in the Old Testament.

5.2 Core texts (a): The covenant curse in Leviticus 26:25

The blessing and curse of the covenant

Leviticus 26 is the conclusion of the so-called Holiness
Code, the code we find in Leviticus Chapters 17-26. In

this code the stipulations of God's covenant are brought home very clearly to Israel. 'Be holy because I, the LORD your God, am holy' is the recurring refrain of the Holiness Code. At the end of it, just as in all Ancient Near Eastern treaties and covenants, we find a long series of blessings and curses. The blessing section runs through verses 3-13, the curse section through verses 14-45. The curse section exhibits a climactic arrangement: the depiction of the punishments becomes progressively more urgent and threatening. In verse 25 God announces a sword, and this sword will avenge the violation of the covenant. Breaking the covenant calls for vengeance. In this case, God's vengeance clearly has a juridical character. God avenging the [broken] covenant is his vindication of it, which is an act of divine justice. His vengeance is the punishment which the Lord, the Ruler, inflicts upon his unfaithful servants and subjects. Wherever in the Old Testament the vengeance of God is announced to Israel, we are dealing with the just punishment of the one who has allied himself with this people, and not with the caprice or bad temper of an unpredictable deity. The background is his covenant.

Serious but not final

Two things can be said about God's vengeance here. First, it is a serious word. Vengeance is linked (cf. v. 28) with the holy wrath of God. Second, we need to say that this vengeance is not God's last word. God's vengeance which implements the curse of the covenant, does not mean that he now breaks the covenant (v. 44), but precisely that he now insists on a return to it. God's vengeance as his reaction to the people's contempt for his covenant with them does not mean revenge for the sake of revenge, retribution for the sake of retribution,

but discipline with a view to restoration. In both blessing
and curse it is one and the same God who is speaking.
Not vengeance, but his covenant faithfulness, is God's
last word (vv. 44-45): 'I am YHWH.'

5.3 Core texts (b): The song of Moses in Deuteronomy 32

The turning point in the song

The song of Moses is a section of extraordinary significance for the entire Old Testament. In numerous other
Scripture passages one senses the influence of this song.
The song stems from ancient times and has, as it were,
become a national anthem, yet it is a very special one
because again and again it was to be sung as a witness
against Israel, from generation to generation, in the worship services, on occasions of covenant renewal, and so
forth. This song has been burned into the soul of Israel.
And in this very song the prophecy of divine vengeance
plays a central role.

As we saw in Chapter 2, the song of Moses has a clear
structure. In verses 1-6 we get the introduction in which
the theme of God's faithfulness and Israel's unfaithfulness is struck. This theme is elaborated in verses 7-18
with a glance at the history of God and his people. It is
not a positive story (v. 18): 'You deserted the Rock, who
fathered you; you forgot the God who gave you birth.'
The rest of the song sings of judgement. Verses 20-25
describe judgement upon Israel. In verses 26-36 we hear
that God does not fully execute his judgement. He holds
it back. Instead of coming over Israel, judgement blazes
away over Israel's enemies. Three times God's
vengeance and retribution are mentioned (vv. 35,41,43).

The content and the reverse side of vengeance

Why does the vengeance of God burn? Because the measure of scorn, folly and hostility is full. The enemy rises up against God. God's honour is at stake. The enemy – used by God as an instrument of punishment upon Israel – think that their own hand has done all this (v. 27). In spirit this is a replay of the building of the tower of Babel. Besides God's honour, his compassion upon Israel is also at stake, for the enemy is fully intent on the destruction of God's people. At that point the Lord intervenes (v. 35). This act of judicial vengeance at the same time means the liberation of Israel (v. 36). Vengeance equals doing justice to his people. It is the reverse side of redemption. They are, we may say, two sides of the same coin. The vengeance of God consists in the punitive requital of the crimes of the enemy, and as such is a matter of justice. For that reason, too, the song ends with a universal summons to rejoice over the vengeance of God. Vengeance upon the enemy atones for the blood guilt of the enemy and so makes life possible in the land once again. The future vengeance of God is the ground and content of the universal song of praise over God's people: without vengeance there is no future.

5.4 Core texts (c): Nahum's consolation in Nahum 1:2

The background of the prophecy

The entire book of Nahum is set to the dark music of the message of God's vengeance. Nahum's prophecy is directed against Nineveh, the capital of the new Assyrian empire, the residence of rulers like Sennacherib. The New Assyrian empire terrorized with increasing violence the entire Ancient Middle East from the ninth to the end of the seventh century BC – three long centuries. They hauled cartloads of loot from the surrounding lands to Nineveh. They unleashed a flood of suffering upon the world. One may say the Assyrians were the Nazis of the Ancient Middle East. A ruler like Sennacherib was the Hitler of the Ancient Middle East.

The prophet Nahum lived and prophesied at a time when the tyrannical world power of Asshur was unbroken, perhaps even at its pinnacle (presumably around 663 BC). As never before in history, a cruel yoke pressed down upon the nations: a strangling by the lion Asshur (2:12). Asshur plundered and ravaged the world in order to fill its den like a lion. At that time even Egypt was conquered by Assyria. After the elimination of Egypt all hope was gone, there was no rival power left. It was Assyria alone that ruled the world. When in this situation the prophet opens his mouth to speak, his prophecy is concentrated solely on one thing: God's vengeance. The Lord is coming to judge. No human can be of help any longer. Yet this injustice, which cries to high heaven, will not triumph, for the Avenger is YHWH! This is not false prophecy poisoned by hatred and nationalism, as some commentators think. It has nothing to do with nationalism, but everything to do with hope in times of extreme distress.

The gong beat in the prophecy

Three times we read: God is the Avenger (Nahum 1:2-3). Like the beat of a gong, it opens the prophecy. The book of Nahum carries a clench-fisted prophecy of the eradication of evil to those who have lost all hope. On this God, the God of vengeance, one can set one's hope – on him who, in his fury and jealousy, sides with the oppressed against a power that is so sinister that it even plots against God (1:11). It is because of God's vengeance that festivals of deliverance can be celebrated. In essence this theology of God's revenge against his enemies is a theology of hope. Nahum 1 therefore ends with rejoicing (v. 15).

5.5 Core texts (d): The blossoming wilderness in Isaiah 35

The link with Isaiah 34

The final text we will look at is closely linked with the chapter which precedes it: Isaiah 34. The two chapters together (Isaiah 34 and 35) are sometimes called Isaiah's little apocalypse. The link, or the hinge, between the two chapters consists in the message of the vengeance of God. The theme of Isaiah 34 is God's vengeance, God's lawsuit on behalf of Zion (v. 8). Judgement passes over the earth, in particular over Edom. Isaiah 35, however, is the absolute opposite of Isaiah 34. Isaiah 35 is light, whereas Isaiah 34 is dark. Isaiah 35 pictures for us a world filled with joy, blossoms, restoration, harmony and life. Is there any room for vengeance and retribution in this setting?

The central place of vengeance

Let us take a closer look at Isaiah 35. First the curtain opens on a happily blossoming and rejoicing wilderness (vv. 1-2), then the summons to banish hopelessness is sounded (vv. 3-4a), along with the message that God is coming in vengeance to save his people (4b). Salvation is sealed with and illustrated by the promise of deliverance from all

physical handicaps (5-6a). This promise is in turn linked
with a renewed description of the wilderness, which at the
same time explains the marvellous vitality exhibited in
verses 1-2 (6b-7). Thus God's coming (4), accompanied by
a summons (3-4a) and a promise   (5-6a), is framed in a
sparkling setting (1-2, 6b-7). Verses 8-10 link up with it by
a threefold 'there': all at once a highway becomes visible in
the blossoming wilderness. Step by step we are told what
kind of highway it is, for whom it is intended, and where
it leads. The final destination is Zion (10). The note of joy
with which the prophecy begins and ends is a dominant
theme throughout the whole chapter.

The people upon whom God's vengeance is executed,
for what reason, and when and how it all happened –
this is left unsaid. It is not necessary to mention it: half a
word is enough for the audience. The word 'vengeance'
is a signal. Now things are put right: a reversal is taking
shape in a dead-end situation; the oppressor will not
escape his just punishment and God's people will be lib-
erated. It is characteristic of the way the Old Testament
speaks of God's vengeance that right in the middle of a
prophetic vision concerning the approaching time of salvation this vengeance can thus have its own place. In the
serene, harmonious portrayal of the glorious joy and
peace that is on its way, the proclamation of the
vengeance of God does not sound as a dissonant note.
On the contrary: vengeance is even given a decisive position here. If God does not come (and on account of the
enemy's deadly oppression it is a coming in vengeance),
there is no longer any hope.

The message of divine vengeance gives strength to
those who are exhausted (vv. 3-4a), and opens the way
to the future (vv. 8-9). It gives impetus to everlasting joy
(v. 10), which does not so much arise on account of the
downfall of the oppressor (in Is. 35 there is not even a

trace of *Schadenfreude*), but arises especially on account of the restoration of the oppressed (cf. Deut. 32:43). Indeed, it is fundamentally joy in God (Is. 29:19-24). In the wake of God's coming in vengeance, the fetters fall away (v. 3), that which restricts life is removed (vv. 5-6a), and the wilderness blossoms (vv. 1-2, 6b-7). What was dead begins to live (both nature and people), and in the midst of this magnificent scene of vivification there is the vengeance of God.

5.6 The context of the vengeance of God in the Old Testament

Vengeance as a function of kingship and judgeship

We have now considered various passages, looking as it were at the colours of a painting with which the Old Testament message of God's vengeance is depicted. But what is the frame of this painting? Let us briefly indicate this in four points.

First, God's vengeance is a function of God's kingship and role as judge. The kingship of God undoubtedly belongs to the basic pattern of the revelation of God in the Old Testament. In all sorts of ways there is mention of God's royal rule – in Old Testament history, in the Psalms, and in prophecy. When this God, who is king, is said to avenge himself, the reference can no longer be to a bad temper, tyrannical caprice, or an explosion of rancour. God's vengeance is royal vengeance. When he executes vengeance, he does so as the highest authority executing punitive judgements. This royal action of vengeance is directed against those who assail God's majesty by the violation of his honour, his justice, or his people. The king is also a judge. To govern and to

administer justice are inseparable acts. He helps the
widow, the orphan and the stranger to obtain justice. The
vengeance of the Royal Judge is the ultimate hope of the
wretched and the devout who can no longer expect anything from eathly judges. If he does not avenge them,
there is no longer any justice on earth (Ps. 58).

Vengeance happens within the covenant

Second, God's vengeance is not realized in the context of
hatred, fury and rancour, but in the context of the
covenant. This is repeatedly made clear from a multi-
plicity of texts: God's vengeance is a warranted reaction
against a breach of covenant.

Vengeance, holiness and justice

Third, God's vengeance is closely related to his holiness.
This is evident from various passages in which God's
vengeance occurs. God, being a holy God, cannot tolerate the breaking of his covenant, injustice, or the
desecration of his name. God's vengeance is holy
vengeance, the vengeance of a holy King. God's
vengeance is at the same time ancillary to his justice, the
goal of which is redemption, restoration and all-around
well-being. To attain that goal, justice can employ the
instrument of vengeance.

Divine vengeance as a source of joy and hope

Fourth, the fact that there is divine vengeance means that
there still remains judgement in a world full of injustice.
God's vengeance provides for the despairing a window
to the future and hope for the oppressed: 'The fact that
ultimately God does not leave evil unpunished is the

primary source of comfort for the countless people in our history who have been robbed and deceived.' (A.S. van der Woude) That knowledge also keeps people from taking the law into their own hands. The promise that in the end God's vengeance will eliminate all evil is a source of joy and gives a reason for praise.

5.7 The God of vengeance in the New Testament

Does Jesus reject vengeance?

Finally, we will trace what we have learned from the Old Testament into the New. Scholars, appealing to Luke 4:18-22, have occasionally stated that Jesus rejects the entire notion of vengeance. When in the synagogue at Nazareth Jesus announces the time of the great fulfilment, he ends his reading from Isaiah 61 with the line about 'the year of the Lord's favour' (Lk. 4:18-19). Jesus omits the line about 'the day of vengeance of our God', which in Isaiah 61 comes immediately after and is inseparably bound up with the preceding line. Coming as it does in the middle of the verse, we can hardly attribute this break to chance. Jesus deliberately refrains from speaking of the day of vengeance. This does not mean, however, that he rejects vengeance. The truth is that the day of vengeance is not 'abolished' by Jesus, but 'delayed'. The present is the time of grace in which the bridegroom is present (Lk. 5:34) and the Gospel is preached to all (Lk. 4:43). But some day the vengeance of God will come (see Lk. 18:1-8 and 21:22). The passage in Luke 4:18f. must not be explained antithetically (i.e. the New Testament opposes and contradicts the Old) but salvation-historically (i.e. the New Testament is in line with the Old).

God's vengeance and sanctification

In the entire New Testament it is presupposed that the God and Father of our Lord Jesus Christ is also the God of vengeance. In 1 Thessalonians 4:6 Paul emphatically states that God is an avenger. This in fact adds force to Paul's exhortation to believers to live a holy life (1 Thes. 4:2-6). The sense of God's vengeance also keeps believers from taking the law into their own hands (Rom. 12:19). 'Vengeance is mine,' says the Lord. In the execution of vengeance God wants to use the government, which as an 'agent of God' must also be his 'agent of wrath' (Rom. 13:4).

God's vengeance and the hope of the future

In the New Testament the message of God's vengeance is especially orientated towards the future (cf. 2 Thes. 1:5-10). At the second coming of the Lord Jesus, vengeance will be executed upon the wicked who refused to obey the Gospel. The parable of the unjust judge in Luke 18:1-8 is worth mentioning here. Finally, and above all, in the book of Revelation we read the cry for the public manifestation of God's vengeance, which occurs unmistakably in the context of justice. His vengeance is the outcome of his judgement in the judicial case of the saints. This is what the souls under the altar cry for (6:10). In 19:2 we hear the echo of that cry. The hope of the ancient Song of Moses (Deut. 32) is fulfilled: 'Hallelujah! Salvation and glory and power belong to our God, for true and just are his judgements. He has condemned the great prostitute, who corrupted the earth by her adulteries. He has avenged on her the blood of his servants.'

The message of God's vengeance gives profound comfort to believers. All injustice which is never redressed, all oppression and opposition, all insults, fear and despair – God puts an end to them. The problem of evil is completely resolved in the final verdict of God's vengeance. Only after the judgement upon and the fall of the great prostitute can the feast of the Lamb and the bride begin – and it will remain for ever without being disturbed (19:6-10).

Questions

1. Discuss the following statement: 'When Simon Wiesenthal describes the motive for his lifelong work as "searching for justice and not for revenge", he means the same as the Old Testament concept of revenge.'

2. How is it possible to enjoy the revenge of God – to which Moses' song in Deuteronomy calls?

3. Do you think people preached more on passages from Nahum during the time of the Second World War?

4. How does the knowledge about God's revenge affect our faith and our daily life?

5. Is it possible that the following opinions are both true at the same time?
   a. There is too little preaching on the passages about revenge
   b. There should not be too much preaching on the passages about revenge.

Bibliography

Dietrich, W., 'Rache. Erwägungen zu einem alttesta-mentlichen Thema', *Evangelische Theologie* 36 (1976), 450-472.

McKeating, H., 'Vengeance is Mine. A Study of the Pursuit of Vengeance in the Old Testament', *Expository Times* 74 (1963), 239-245.

Mendenhall, G., *The Tenth Generation*, Baltimore 1973.

Merz, E., *Die Blutrache bei den Israeliten*, Leipzig 1916.

Musvosvi, J.N., *The Concept of Vengeance in the Book of Revelation in its Old Testament and Near Eastern Context*, Andrews University 1987.

Peels, H.G.L., *The Vengeance of God. The Meaning of the Root NQM and the Function of the NQM-texts in the Context of Divine Revelation in the Old Testament (Oudtestamentische Studiën XXXI)*, Leiden, 1995.

Peels, H.G.L., lemma .81 (nqm), in: W.A. VanGemeren (ed.), *New International Dictionary of Old Testament Theology and Exegesis* Volume III, Carlisle 1997, 154-157.

Peels, H.G.L., 'God's Throne in Elam: The Historical Background and Literary Context of Jeremiah 49:34-39', in: J.C. de Moor / H.F. van Rooij (eds.), *Past, Present, Future. The Deuteronomistic History and the Prophets (Oudtestamentische Studiën XLIV)*, Leiden 2000, 216-229.

Peels, H.G.L., *'Voed het oud vertrouwen weder'. De Godsopenbaring bij Nahum* (Apeldoornse Studies 28), Kampen 1993.

Pitard, W.T., 'Vengeance,' in *The Anchor Bible Dictionary*. Volume 6, New York 1992, 786-787.

6

The Call for God's Revenge in the Old Testament

6.1 The imprecatory prayer: a stumbling-block

Some examples

To many people the imprecatory and cursing prayers, frequently present in the Old Testament, are perhaps even more of a stumbling-block than the words about God's revenge (see the previous chapter). This is not surprising when we read the sometimes horrifying phrasing: '...happy is he...who seizes your infants and dashes them against the rocks', as Psalm 137:8-9 states. Or Psalm 58:10: 'The righteous will be glad when they are avenged, when they bathe their feet in the blood of the wicked' (cf. Ps. 68:23 and Rev. 14:20). Psalm 59:13a reads: '...consume them in wrath, consume them till they are no more.' How can this be combined with the Lord's prayer on the cross: 'Father, forgive them, for they do not know what they are doing' (Lk. 23:34) and his words in the Sermon on the Mount: 'But I tell you: Love your enemies and pray for those who persecute you...' (Mt. 5:44)? Furthermore, does the apostle Paul not clearly say in Romans 12:14: 'Bless those who persecute you; bless and do not curse'? Are the imprecatory prayers in the Old Testament really inspired by the Holy Spirit? What shall we do with them?

Antithetical explanation

Marcion, the well-known and notorious heretic from the middle of the second century AD, knew what to do with them (see also Chapter 1). He is the author of a work entitled *The antitheses* in which he detects and enlarges on all sorts of possible distinctions between the Old and the New Testaments. The result is that he throws overboard the whole Old Testament. The God of the New Testament is a different, foreign God, who sends his Son Jesus to save humankind from the power of the severe, frigid god of the Old Testament. Marcion thinks that the Old and the New Testaments are related to each other as justice, revenge and war are to love, forgiveness and mercy. Marcion's range of thought still has its impact today. It is perceptible in many commentaries on the Bible, which explain the Old Testament cursing prayers as a sign of inferior spiritual life. The religion of the Old Testament – as one German commentator states – was a *Nationalreligion* (national religion), which needed to be replaced by the *reine Menschenreligion* (pure humane religion), which is Christianity. The Old Testament was considered to be on a lower level than the New. This we call the antithetical explanation.

The explanation of psychology

Others are searching for a solution using psychology. They try to gloss the imprecatory prayers. These are of course basically unacceptable, they state, yet understandable in an historical way considering the times of need in which the prayers were said. One can see that the psalmists were no saints. In the imprecatory prayers we sense the passion of the Bedouin. In particular, former German exegetes give way to their anti-Semitic feelings by attributing the prayers to the old national *Judengeist* (the 'Jewish soul/mood'), which is filled with hatred. We shall not waste more words on their opinion.

Yet scholars who write from within a very different sort of tradition, and in a different spirit, can also be very critical about the cursing prayers. Some sense in them the fiery passion of the desert, which is understandable, yet not to be imitated. The idea of these scholars is that in the same way as we do not imitate David in all his ways, though he was a man of God, neither should we pick up these psalms. There is too much unlimited and unconquered human nature in them, too much passion, too much anger. The above-mentioned Old Testament scholar Theodoor Vriezen is an example of this sort of critic. On the phenomenon of the cursing prayers he remarks that he does not want to do without them in the collection of Old Testament writings, yet he cannot attribute to them the character of God's message and his revelation, neither does he sense the work of the Holy Spirit, who is revealed in Jesus Christ. To him the imprecatory psalms and prayers are very human and they do not always contain sanctified ideas. He thinks they are far remote from Christ's prayer for his enemies on the cross, and from the essence of the Lord's Prayer (*An Outline of Old Testament Theology*, Oxford 1958, pp. 88 and 305).

On closer view we notice in neither the antithetical nor the psychological explanation any effort to understand the Old Testament imprecatory prayers in their own nature and their own context. In this chapter we will try to do them more justice than these interpretations.

6.2 No marginal phenomenon

Forms of imprecatory prayer

The imprecatory prayer is not a marginal phenomenon in the Old Testament. On numerous occasions the prayer for revenge on the enemy is heard. This may happen in different forms. In the first place as an actual *prayer* to God: 'O LORD, the God who avenges, O God who avenges, shine forth. Rise up, O Judge of the earth; pay back to the proud what they deserve' (Ps. 94:1-2). In the second place as a *wish*: 'May those who seek my life be disgraced and put to shame; may those who plot my ruin be turned back in dismay. May they be like chaff before the wind, with the angel of the Lord driving them away' (Ps. 35:4-5). In the third place in the shape of an *expectation* or a *promise*; thus we read concerning 'the wicked': '...their swords will pierce their own hearts, and their bows will be broken' (Ps. 37:15).

Separate cursing psalms?

The curse, imprecation or prayer of revenge is part of many psalms. Some scholars use the term 'cursing psalms', but this is not right. In vain we look for specific psalms of revenge or curse. It is striking that these elements are even present in hymns, royal psalms, wisdom psalms and songs of thanksgiving. More than a hundred psalms contain a sort of prayer of revenge in one way or another – and this is two thirds of the whole book!

Elsewhere in the Old Testament

Outside the book of the Psalms, in the rest of the Old Testament, there are prayers of revenge as well. When Joab murders Abner, David cries out:

I and my kingdom are for ever innocent before the LORD concerning the blood of Abner son of Ner. May his blood fall upon the head of Joab and upon all his father's house! May Joab's house never be without someone who has a running sore or leprosy or who leans on a crutch or who falls by the sword or who lacks food (2 Sam. 3:28-29).

When king Joash kills Zechariah, the son of Jehoiada, the victim cries: 'May the LORD see this and call you to account' (2 Chr. 24:22). The prophet Jeremiah prays concerning his adversaries:

So give their children over to famine; hand them over to the power of the sword. Let their wives be made childless and widows; let their men be put to death, their young men slain by the sword in battle. Let a cry be heard from their houses when you suddenly bring invaders against them, for they have dug a pit to capture me and have hidden snares for my feet. But you know, O LORD, all their plots to kill me. Do not forgive their crimes or blot out their sins from your sight. Let them be overthrown before you; deal with them in the time of your anger (Jer. 18:21-23; cf. Neh. 4:4-5).

Read as well 2 Kings 1:10,12; Amos 7:17; Jeremiah 15:15 and 17:18. We are not dealing here with some immoral ravings of a bloodthirsty psalmist or of a prophet with personal feelings of hatred, but with a structural element of the relationship between God and humankind in the Old Testament. In order to understand the prayer of revenge, we must take into account three major aspects: its background, its context and its intention.

6.3 The background of the prayer of revenge

The Ancient Near Eastern traditions

In the first place the prayer for revenge or for a curse must be set against the background of the Ancient Near Eastern tradition of cursing. By 'curse' we do not, of course, mean blasphemy, but a curse put on someone. Mankind in ancient times had a totally different opinion about these things from our own view today. We think a word is 'just a word'. In the ancient world, however, a word was a reality, something which was active. The seriousness and the reality of a curse were dreaded. It was more than 'just a word'.

In all sorts of areas of life curses were used as a normal thing. The oath was a form of self-imprecation (cf. the expression in 1 Sam. 14:44: 'May God deal with me, be it ever so severely, if...'). In court the curse was used as a means of affecting the unknown guilty. Thieves, people who were dishonest and did not bring back what they had borrowed, defilers of a grave: let them be cursed! In the Ancient Near Eastern laws there are series of curses in the same way as we have penalty clauses. Curses were added to treaties and covenants as a way of sanctioning the demands on the parties involved. Curses were written on graves, on buildings, on boundary stones to secure them, etc. In everyday life curses were used: to protect things, to safeguard them, as a guarantee. The expressed curses were often very conventional and stereotyped.

The curse in Israel

In Israel the situation was no different. The Israelites evaluated words of curse and blessing in a very different way from the ways they are understood today. The curse in the Old Testament had real power and was therefore dreaded. It can be compared with a mortar-shell which is directed precisely and explodes on the determined spot where it causes immense chaos. It is a power of corruption and destruction, a power to scorch and to wither. The conviction that a word of curse was powerful is very realistic; read for instance Leviticus 5:1; Judges 17:2; and the law on jealousy in Numbers 5. Yet the idea that it is a sort of magical conviction (as if the curse should automatically have a particular result) is incorrect. Israelites knew very well that the curse is a divine weapon and that God will execute it (cf. Judg. 9:57; Deut. 28:20).

They were not startled when they heard a prayer for a curse in the psalms, for they were too accustomed to the use of cursing expressions in daily life. Still less did they consider it to be an immoral utterance of hatred or of feelings of revenge. In Israel the curse worked as an efficient means in the context of economy, court or politics. Read for instance Genesis 24:41; Ezekiel 17:13; Zechariah 5:3; Deuteronomy 27:11-26; 29:12,14; 1 Kings 8:31-32.

Legitimate and illegitimate

It is important to realize that the Old Testament world made a clear distinction between cursing in a legitimate and an illegitimate way. Some examples are: 'Anyone who curses his father or mother must be put to death' (Ex. 21:17). Job says: 'I have not allowed my mouth to sin by invoking a curse against his life' (31:30; cf. Hos. 10:4). The illegitimate curse was improper and punishable. In the Psalms the enemy is reproved for illegitimate cursing (Ps. 10:7; 59:12; 62:4; 109:17,28). The psalmist does not fall into the same sin. He does not curse his adversary. With the prayer for a curse he acts in a different way: he places justice against injustice, the appeal for God against the curse of the godless enemy. He himself renounces personal revenge.

6.4 The context of the prayer of revenge

Subject and object

The prayer for revenge and for a curse must be understood in its own context, which we trace when we notice who is speaking in the psalms (the subject) and who is the psalmist's enemy (the object). The subject of these psalms is not just a random person; it is the 'poor', the 'righteous', the 'miserable' or the 'humble' who pray. These words in the Old Testament indicate a special relationship with God. The 'poor' are helpless and wait for God's help. They have no other help. They are totally dependent on God's legal assistance and his mercy. The Lord 'secures justice for the poor and upholds the cause of the needy' (Ps. 140:12; cf. Ps. 9:4; 68:5; 82:3). An important passage is Exodus 22:22-24: 'Do not take advantage of a widow or an orphan. If you do and they cry out to me, I will certainly hear their cry. My anger will be aroused, and I will kill you with the sword; your wives will become widows and your children fatherless' (cf. Prov. 22:22-23). This is what happens in the prayer of revenge: the poor cry out to God.

Opposite the special subject of the prayer for a curse is the special object: the 'enemy', the 'godless', the 'adversary'. In the psalms we do not clearly see the identity of the enemy. No names are mentioned, specific indications are absent. Yet there is a picture of people without God which is repeated. It is constantly clear that they are breaking the rules of the covenant. They provoke the believer and even want to separate him from God. They are oppressing God's people. The enemies in the psalms are a picture of ultimate wickedness and godlessness. One can say that the Evil One is reflected in their deeds. The psalms are dealing with more than a controversy between David or another psalmist and his personal or national enemies. Part of the spiritual battle between God's Kingdom and the anti-powers is revealed.

The covenant

The poor against their enemies, the just against the wicked – in these tensions the prayer of revenge takes place. Both subject and object belong to the people with whom God has a special covenant relationship. The person who prays cries out to the God of the covenant. The use of possessive pronouns in the psalms is characteristic. Read for instance Psalm 94:5: 'They crush *your* people, O LORD; they oppress *your* inheritance', and verse 14: 'For the LORD will not reject *his* people; he will never forsake *his* inheritance' (italics mine). Life in its totality – not only religion – is included in the covenant, including the economy, justice and politics. The covenant forms a rich blessing, a great treasure. The Israelites could not be too careful in dealing with it. Yet the wicked harm the covenant and therefore they must be punished.

Curses and blessings

When God made a covenant with his people, it was confirmed by both blessings and curses (Lev. 26; Deut. 27 and 28). Obedience and disobedience concerning the rules of covenantal life result in salvation or doom, mercy or judgement, blessing or curse (cf. 2 Chr. 15:13). These words of life and death, of blessing and curse, were constantly impressed upon the people by the cult (Deut. 31:12-13).

The people even agreed with the blessings and curses in an official ceremony: 'Then all the people shall say, "Amen!"' (Deut. 27:11-26; Josh. 8:30-35). Those who break the covenant will be cut off from the people, because their disobedience threatens the whole covenant community.

In this context the prayers including curses are heard. They are in the same line, as it were, as the curses of the covenant, which is harmed by the raging of the wicked. They are not the ones who are destroyed, but the righteous are – and no one intervenes! So the psalmist prays and joins in God's own words. This cannot be characterized as pouring out one's feelings of revenge; the psalmist actually takes up God's own covenant curse for the wicked when he uses the traditionally shaped expressions of curse. The enemy breaks God's covenant and is therefore, by definition, under God's curse. Read for instance Lamentations 3:64-65: 'Pay them back what they deserve, O LORD, for what their hands have done. Put a veil over their hearts, and may your curse be on them!' The background of the psalmist's prayer for the curse of a national enemy is God's promise to Abraham: 'I will bless those who bless you, and whoever curses you I will curse' (Gen. 12:3).

Again and again we notice that the prayer for a curse is not a marginal phenomenon that can be left out as a kind of 'accident', but is deeply embedded in the basic structure of the Old Testament. It is related to the most important ideas of Israelite religion.

6.5 The intention of the prayer of revenge

The preservation of justice

When we ask what the essence of the psalmists' prayer for revenge is, we get to the third and most important feature of it. Is the main thing the fulfilment of revenge-fulness? Nowhere is this made clear. In the first place they are concerned with deliverance and the restoration of justice. Their prayer for revenge is an appeal to the God of the covenant to intervene and to do justice to his own covenantal words by delivering his faithful servants and punishing those who break the covenant. A good example is 1 Samuel 24:12,15 in which David prays for 'revenge', in his case with Saul: 'May the LORD judge between you and me. And may the LORD avenge the wrongs you have done to me ... May the LORD be our judge and decide between us. May he consider my cause and uphold it...' David does not exceed the limit, which Saul acknowledges: '"You are more righteous than I", he said. "You have treated me well, but I have treated you badly"' (v. 17).

Constantly, legal expressions and ideas are used in the passages where we read curses. Doing justice is of vital importance. When justice has become corrupt, society will be destroyed. In Psalm 94:20 we read about 'a corrupt throne ... that brings on misery by its decrees'. When God will intervene by punishment and revenge, 'Judgement will again be founded on righteousness' (Ps. 94:15). In the prayers of revenge a strong belief is expressed in God as Judge and King, who cannot bear any form of injustice. If there is any emotion which colours the prayer for a curse, it is the anger concerning injustice and the contempt of evil which is harming society. The psalmist resembles Jeremiah, who states (6:11): 'But I am full of the wrath of the LORD'.

The preservation of God's honour

The prayer for revenge is even more far-reaching. God's honour is at stake. The prayer for a curse emerges from the perplexing experience that the blessings and curses of the covenant do not work any more. The wicked flourish, whereas the righteous decline. Pagans triumph, but God's people perish. How is this possible? Is there a God who does justice on earth? In fact, God himself is harmed by the harming of the covenant. In the context of the covenant, mocking and hating the righteous actually touches their God. The enemy who wants to destroy Israel, in fact aims at God (see Ps. 83:5). The psalmist's intention is that God should show his justice. Thus prayers for a curse often end with the hope that the pagans will be aware that God is really God and that he is reigning – read for instance Psalm 58:11; 59:13; 83:18.

God's Kingdom now breaking through

Whoever reads the Old Testament cursings carefully will notice a call for the breakthrough of God's Kingdom by deliverance and revenge. The psalmist's main point is that the Lord is God and that there is no other, that he reigns and that justice is safe in his hands, and that the words of his covenant are true (see Ps. 10:16-18). Frequently God is called King, Judge, Warrior. Read for instance Psalm 94. Parallel to 'the God who avenges' in verse 1, verse 2 says that he is 'judge of the earth'. God the Judge is also the King. Psalm 94 is part of a couple of psalms which sing the praises of God's Kingship (Psalms 93-99). From this King-Judge revenge is required. Our word 'revenge' has a very negative, illegitimate, immoral sound. As we saw in the previous chapter, however, the biblical word revenge sounded very positively in the ears of the Israelites and was mainly a legal term. People can long for this sort of revenge, they can rejoice at it, because it means restoration of justice, deliverance and a future.

It is striking that the psalmist of the Old Testament prays for the revelation of God's Kingship here and now. *'Before our eyes,* make known among the nations that you avenge the outpoured blood of your servants' (Ps. 79:10; italics mine). We must realize that the Old Testament believer had only a very restricted view of life after death and of a possible justification after death – remember the paragraph of the first chapter about the history of revelation. In Old Testament times the frightening issue of whether injustice would reign for ever was a very real one. Yet again and again people held on to the Lord and waited for him: 'For the LORD is our judge, the LORD is our lawgiver, the LORD is our king; it is he who will save us' (Is. 33:22). The expectation of God's revenge even becomes an integrated part of the hope for a different, better future (Ps. 104:35; 149). Once the evil is eradicated root and branch, then God's Kingdom will come for ever. In this way the author of Psalm 137 prays in the words of old prophecies on Edom and Babylon. He takes up, as it were, God's own word of doom on the enemies of his people. The shocking prayer of revenge in Psalm 137:8-9 is preceded by the prophetic words of Isaiah 13:16-18 and 14:22.

Literal or metaphorical

The question arises as to how far the psalmists longed for a literal fulfilment of their prayers for a curse. We must always keep in mind that they used traditional stereotyped language. By means of classical expressions of curse, the psalmist asks for God's intervention. David prays in Psalm 59:13a: 'Consume them in wrath, consume them till they are no more.' The prayer is meant for Saul, who had David's house guarded in order to kill him (v. 1). Yet at the same time David prays in verse 13b: 'Then it will be known to the ends of the earth that God rules over Jacob.' And when David's enemy Saul has perished, he does not sing for joy and perverse delight, but he tears his clothes, mourns and fasts, and writes one of the most moving laments in the Old Testament: 'Your glory, O Israel, lies slain on your heights. How the mighty have fallen!' (2 Sam. 1:17-27). The prayer for a curse pleads for punishment of the enemy, but it does not determine the way in which this will happen.

6.6 Is the prayer of revenge superseded by the New Testament?

False contrasts

To the question of whether the Old Testament prayer of revenge is superseded in the New, or even needs to be condemned, the answer is: no. It is not right to contrast the Old Testament prayer of revenge directly with certain New Testament texts like the prayer of forgiveness on the cross, because they are on a 'different level'. We must constantly bear in mind the specific nature and place of the words in the history of salvation and revelation. It is clear that the prayer of revenge is not condemned in the New Testament, since many imprecatory psalms are cited in it without any problem, like Psalm 2, 35, 69 and 109. Nowhere in the New Testament do writers have any problem with the Old Testament prayer of revenge. Thus Jesus and his disciples sang the 'Hallel', the series containing Psalms 113-118, at the Passover meal. In the final psalm we read three times: 'in the name of the LORD I cut them off' (Ps. 118:10-12).

Love in the Old Testament

Furthermore, we need to realize that the Old Testament forbids revengefulness and orders us to love our neighbour; read in particular Leviticus 19:18 (and the extension of the command to love in verse 34). Compare Exodus 23:4-5; Job 31:29-30; Psalm 7:4-6; Proverbs 17:5,7; 24:17-18; 25:21-22. Striking is the way in which David, the author of many prayers for curses, acts towards Saul, who is the Lord's anointed. David does not want to lift a hand against him (1 Sam. 24:13,18). David sings praises to the Lord when Abigail prevents him from getting charged with blood-guilt and settling his own case (1 Sam. 25:22-26). We cannot play off the Old Testament as the one of justice against the New as the one of love.

Wrath in the New Testament

The New Testament speaks even more seriously about God's wrath, judgement of sin and animosity against him, and about the battle against the powers of darkness. In the New Testament preaching there is even the possibility of *eternal* doom (2 Thes. 1:9). Even in the New Testament we can read a 'prayer for a curse', as in 1 Corinthians 16:22: 'If anyone does not love the Lord – a curse be on him. Come, O Lord!' Also powerful is the repetition of words in Galatians 1:8-9: 'But even if we or an angel from heaven should preach a gospel other than the one we preached to you, let him be eternally condemned!' We mentioned earlier the prayer of the souls under the altar (Rev. 6:10). We may think of Jesus' cursing the fig tree in Matthew 21:19 and Peter's words to Simon Magus in Acts 8:20: 'May your money perish with you...' Full of warning and threat are the 'woes' Jesus proclaims in Luke 11:37-54. In this respect there is no contrast between the Old Testament and the New. Neither is it right to ignore the differences between the two Testaments considering the prayer of revenge, for they are real. We can state that in the New Testament the prayer of revenge is specifically focused.

6.7 The focus of the prayer of revenge in the New Testament

Progress in salvation history

Not only are there less prayers for a curse in the New Testament compared to the Old, also the prayers are changed. They are now closely associated with the proclamation of the Gospel and the coming judgement. All this is related to the great turn in the history of salvation through the coming of Jesus Christ. When he came to earth the world's history had entered a decisive phase. That which was more or less still in darkness, became clear by his coming into the world. All essential things in the Old Testament have been fully developed. The fullness of time and the Kingdom of God have come.

John the Baptist proclaims this message and immediately it has two sides: salvation *and*, in particular, judgement: 'The axe is already at the root of the trees...' (Mt. 3:10-12). John speaks about 'baptising with fire' and the 'burning up ... with unquenchable fire'. In John's preaching it is not clear what place the nations have in this expectation. This becomes clear, however, in the preaching and the work of Jesus. Judgement is executed, but in a different way from John the Baptist's expectations: at Golgotha. This judgement means salvation for all who believe and a total expiation of all their sins. In this time of mercy and grace, the time of God's patience, his message spreads over all the earth. Whoever rebels against it, will be finally judged. The tension between the 'now and here' of God's Kingdom *and* the future of it, which is still to come, determines the place the prayer for a curse in the New Testament (read also the paragraph in the first chapter about the history of salvation).

The 'here and now' of the Kingdom

On the one hand, the Kingdom of God has come. The prayer 'Thy Kingdom come', which was at the heart of the Old Testament prayer for a curse, is fulfilled in a certain way. In it God's justice and honour were at stake. The power of evil seemed to be winning. But in this age the cross of Christ is the definitive and manifest revelation of God's righteousness (Rom. 3:25-26). The curse of the law as the result of all disobedience was put on him (Gal. 3:10,13). Therefore his people are saved once and for all and the evil enemy is defeated (Heb. 2:14). God's judgement is executed in Christ in a fundamental way. This fact changes the urgent and acute prayer for God's intervention and punishment as it was heard in the Old Testament. This may be the main reason why the prayer for a curse is heard less frequently in the New Testament than in the Old.

The 'not yet' of the Kingdom

There is the 'already' and the 'not yet' of the Kingdom of God. His Kingdom has not yet reached its fulfilment. There is still sinning, struggle, battles; believers are attacked, and there is animosity. Yet judgement will come to all who stubbornly reject the Gospel of Christ. This assurance of the final judgement, which the Old Testament believers did not yet have, changes the prayer of revenge. The current time is characterized as the age of God's patience and grace in order that people may repent (Rom. 2:4; 2 Pet. 2:9; 3:9; cf. Rev. 6:11 after 6:10). It is the age of the Gospel spreading everywhere to save people (Jn. 3:17). In the meantime weeds and grain are growing together. Only in the time of harvest the sower is the one who is reaping. In this period the attitude of the believers is determined by the words: 'Bless those who persecute you; bless and do not curse' (Rom. 12:14). Concerning the enemy, the Christian prayer on the one hand means entrusting oneself 'to him who judges justly' (1 Pet. 2:23), and on the other hand it is a prayer for forgiveness and repentance (Acts 7:60; 8:22). This does not diminish the fact that in the New Testament the zeal for God's honour and justice, the guarding of the church's purity and the longing for the total revelation of God's majesty, including the destruction of evil, are also highly prized. That is why the prayer of revenge is still heard in situations of emergency, even though times have changed. It is a prayer led by the Holy Spirit and it is not aimed at a personal enemy, but at the enemies of God. Of lasting value is the prayer for deliverance from the Evil One, the complete destruction of darkness and the coming of God's Kingdom. This is the meaning of question and answer 123 in the Heidelberg Catechism:

What is the second petition? 'Thy kingdom come.' That is: so govern us by thy Word and Spirit that we may more and more submit ourselves unto thee. Uphold and increase thy church. Destroy the works of the devil, every power that raises itself against thee, and all wicked schemes thought up against thy holy Word, until the full coming of thy kingdom in which thou shalt be all in all (cf. question and answer 52, and the Belgic Confession of Faith, article 37).

Questions

1. Why is it important to realize that the background of the imprecatory psalms is not primarily the utterance of personal feelings, but the covenant of God and his people?

2. Someone once said that we can only read an imprecatory psalm in very special, sanctified moments, and that most of us can never, others seldom, and only the real saints can sing these psalms in full confidence of mind. What do you think of this?

3. What can we deduce from the remarkable fact that in so many psalms there is a battle against 'enemies'?

4. Do you think a preacher can let the congregation sing the Old Testament psalms which contain a prayer for a curse and for revenge?

5. Do we know exactly what we mean when we pray 'Thy Kingdom come'? In answering this question, take note of the passage from 2 Thessalonians 1:7-9.

Bibliography

Bernardino, N.C., *A reconsideration of 'imprecations' in the Psalms*, Grand Rapids 1986.

Brongers, H.A., 'Die Rache- und Fluchpsalmen im Alten Testament', *Oudtestamentische Studiën* 13 (1963), 21-42.

Dhanaraj, D., *Theological Significance of the Motif of Enemies in Selected Psalms of Individual Lament* (Orientalia Biblica et Christiana 4), Glückstadt 1992.

Janowski, B., 'Dem Löwen gleich, gierig nach Raub. Zum Feindbild in den Psalmen', *Evangelische Theologie* 55 (1995), 155-173.

Lohfink, N. (ed.), *Gewalt und Gewaltlosigkeit im Alten Testament*, Freiburg 1983.

Peels, H.G.L., *The Vengeance of God. The Meaning of the Root NQM and the Function of the NQM-texts in the Context of Divine Revelation in the Old Testament* (Oudtestamentische Studiën XXXI), Leiden, 1995.

Peels, H.G.L., '"Gelukkig hij die de uw kinderen zal grijpen". Hermeneutische en bijbels-theologische positionering van de oudtestamentische vloekbede', *Acta Theologica* 22/1 (2002), 117-134.

Peels, H.G.L., '"Drinken zùlt gij!" Plaats en betekenis van Jeremia's volkenprofetieën (Jer. 46-51)', *Theologia Reformata* 44/3 (2001), 218-233.

Sauer, G., *Die strafende Vergeltung Gottes in den Psalmen. Eine frömmigkeitsgeschichtliche Untersuchung*. I. Teil, Erlangen 1961.

Van der Velden, F., *Psalm 109 und die Aussagen zur Feindschädigung in den Psalmen* (SBB 37), Stuttgart 1997.

Zenger, E., *Ein Gott der Rache? Feindpsalmen verstehen*, Freiburg/Basel/Wien 1994.

God's Anger in the Old Testament

7.1 Anger of human beings and gods

The concept of 'anger'

In modern language there is a whole range of terms to express different aspects of the concept of anger: fury, wrath, rage, aggression, etc. Anger is a very fundamental emotion. People react when their honour, property or interests are injured. They react to injustice or violence, pain or sorrow, and so on. In the second century AD the Greek doctor and philosopher Galenus developed the theory that the differences in character and temperament are caused by a different mix of bodily fluids: phlegm, blood (sanguine), yellow bile (choler), and black bile (melancholy). The predominance of one fluid defines one's character; thus there are four different sorts of people: those with a phlegmatic (calm, stoic), sanguine (joyful, capricious), choleric (hot-tempered), or melancholic (gloomy, pessimistic) temperament. Galenus thought the inclination to anger was a characteristic of the choleric. Yet people with another sort of character know about anger as well, as we see around us.

Human anger

The Bible speaks less about human than about divine anger. Human anger is not always negative. We read about some 'holy' anger, like that of Moses, who descends Mount Sinai and sees Israel dancing around the golden calf (Ex. 32:19,22). Another example is Elisha, who tells Joash to take arrows and strike the ground (2 Kgs. 13:19). A human being can also be full of God's anger, like the prophet Jeremiah (6:11; 15:17). King David is extremely angry when he hears Nathan's story of a rich person who takes the poor man's lamb (2 Sam. 12:5).

In general, however, human anger is a negative thing. Often it is selfish, originating from the wrong motives. In his anger a person loses his sense of proportion and the anger undermines his self-control. The uncontrolled rage expresses itself in irresponsible behaviour. In particular the wisdom literature warns against it: 'Anger is cruel and fury overwhelming' (Prov. 27:4). 'A fool gives full vent to his anger, but a wise man keeps himself under control' (Prov. 29:11). Therefore we must neither befriend 'hot-tempered' people nor 'associate with one easily angered' (Prov. 22:24). We should mind our words: 'A gentle answer turns away wrath, but a harsh word stirs up anger' (Prov. 15:1). In a similar way Paul writes in the letter to the Ephesians (4:26) that no one should sin in his anger (cf. Col. 3:8). James states: 'Everyone should be quick to listen, slow to speak and slow to become angry, for man's anger does not bring about the righteous life that God desires' (1:19-20). Jesus Christ even puts anger on the same level as murder (Mt. 5:22).

Furious gods

Gods in the Ancient Near East did not take heed of the wise instructions mentioned above. The stories in ancient mythology seem to be rather those which tell us about the gods' drunkenness, sexual excesses, fears and furious outbursts. In the Babylonian Atrahasis-epic (see also Chapter 4) the god Enlil decides to cause the deluge because of the noise human beings make. He is furious because he cannot sleep. Later on he sees that the human Atrahasis escapes from the deluge by boat, and he is out of control because of his rage. The Egyptian gods have problems with their self-control as well. The god Seth is known as the 'furious one', whose anger is irrational and chaotic. The human race would have been extinguished by the furious, bloodthirsty goddess Hathor if the other gods had not prevented her at the last minute. In one of the Hittite myths the god Telepinu becomes so extremely angry that he is not able to put his shoes on the right feet before he flounces out. In his fury, which has no apparent reason, he brings drought and famine to the whole world. He becomes even more furious when he is stung by a bee that wants to wake him from sleep. The Canaanite god Baal becomes extremely angry when the chief god El tells him to bow before the messengers of the god Yam; instead, he takes a knife and hits out. All in all, a very easily irritated company. In that world the God of Israel revealed himself. How is his anger discussed in the Old Testament?

7.2 Terminology and metaphors in the Old Testament

Terminology

The Hebrew language contains many words which express the idea of anger. In one and the same chapter we may find a great variety of terms, as in Deuteronomy

29. The most frequently used Hebrew word for anger literally meant 'nose' or 'nostrils'. The nose has more to do with anger than with smell: 'Smoke rose from his nostrils' (Ps. 18:8). Another Hebrew word alludes to anger as a burning fire; it can be translated as 'wrath' (Ps. 89:46). A third term refers to the outburst of anger as a storm which blows up. Yet another word contains the aspect of deep indignation. One can offend God, which is similar to raising his anger (Deut. 32:19,21). Often God's anger is compared with the action of fire.

Strikingly, words for anger which are connected with a name of God (the anger of...) are almost always used together with the name YHWH (Yahweh, Lord), but not with the word 'God' (*El* or *Elohim*) or 'Lord' (*Adonai*). The name YHWH is the covenant name *par excellence*. With that name God has related himself specifically to his people, Israel. And that very name is used when an author in the Bible specifies whose anger is referred to. In general, the anger of God hints at his disciplinary action in judgement: anger is 'poured out' (Hos. 5:10), it is 'brought down' (Is. 66:15). Besides, the Old Testament speaks of God's anger as a manifestation of his feelings; he reacts to sin and injustice; anger may 'rise' (Ps. 18:8) or 'burn' (Deut. 6:15).

The Greek translation of the Old Testament, the Septuagint, had at its disposal mainly three Greek words for translating the Hebrew 'anger'. Two of them are hardly ever used of gods in Greek literature. The third word, *mènis*, which alludes to grudge or rancour, is the Greek term pre-eminently used for the anger of gods. The Septuagint never uses the word *mènis* for God's anger.The translators apparently clearly realized the difference between God's anger and the general anger of the gods.

Metaphors

Different metaphors are used to make God's anger more visible. Frequently the metaphor of a fire is used: 'For a fire has been kindled by my wrath, one that burns to the realm of death below. It will devour the earth and its harvests and set on fire the foundations of the mountains' (Deut. 32:22). We read the opposite in Hosea 5: 'I will pour out my wrath on them like a flood of water' (v. 10). Both fire and water are metaphors for God's anger in Isaiah 30:27-33. Jeremiah uses another metaphor: 'See, the storm of the LORD will burst out in wrath, a whirlwind swirling down' (23:19). In his action of anger God is compared with a hero who prepares himself for battle (Is. 59:16-19), with a blacksmith who is melting metals and blowing the fire (his fiery wrath) in the furnace (Ezek. 22:17-22), or with someone who is treading the winepress (Is. 63:1-6).

Often the expression 'the cup of wrath' is used, which God or the prophet offer to the nations to drink. The cup is filled with 'wine', which means judgement and wrath. It must be drunk to the last drop. 'In the hand of the LORD is a cup full of foaming wine mixed with spices; he pours it out, and all the wicked of the earth drink it down to its very dregs' (Ps. 75:8). Yet God can also withdraw the cup: 'Therefore hear this, you afflicted one, made drunk, but not with wine ... See, I have taken out of your hand the cup that made you stagger; from that cup, the goblet of my wrath, you will never drink again' (Is. 51:21-22).

7.3 The anger of the Lord

Real, but not essential

The way in which the Bible speaks about the anger of God makes clear that it is a reality. It is not just a metaphor; God is not angry in name, but in reality. The Lord is a God who is emotionally involved in a divine way in the ups and downs of the world and of human beings. Throughout the Scriptures we encounter the seriousness of God's anger in an increasing way. For good reason the author of Psalm 7 confesses: 'God is a righteous judge, a God who expresses his wrath every day' (v. 11). The prophet Nahum even says that the Lord 'is filled with wrath' (1:2). If people think God cannot be angry (Zeph. 1:12), they are completely wrong. In this matter the Old Testament prophets clashed with the false ones, who only prophesied peace (Jer. 6:14-15; 14:13). Even today we must guard against minimalizing the reality of God's judgement and anger.

At the same time we can say that anger is not an essential characteristic of God in the same way as he is the holy God, the jealous One, the loving and faithful One. The Bible says God is love, but never 'God is anger'. Long ago Calvin stated that anger is not a disposition of God. That is not the case with some of the gods surrounding Israel, for instance the Egyptian god Seth. In his essence he is a furious god. The same applies to the Graeco-Roman goddesses who bear the name 'Erinys', which means 'furies'. They are constituted by anger, which they express in taking revenge. What a contrast with Israel's God, who is alive! Being angry is not his essential work, but his 'strange' work (Is. 28:21). Firmly anchored within Israel's confession of faith are the words that God is slow to anger (Ex. 34:6). The Lord loves to forgive and to be gracious (Is. 30:18). He does not like to be angry: 'For he does not willingly bring affliction or grief to the children of men' (Lam. 3:33). That is why the people ask '...will you always be angry? Will your wrath continue for ever?' (Jer. 3:5). The Lord had even established the whole institution of atonement to guard his people against the action of his anger (see the book of Leviticus). And often the Old Testament describes how God withholds or softens his anger (Ex. 32:12-14; Is. 54:7-8; Hos. 11:8; Mic. 7:18; see also Chapter 9). What a contrast this is with the anger of gods which we meet in ancient mythology, where often the outbursts of a god's anger must be softened by the intervention of other gods.

Anger, holiness and love

Whenever God is angry, he is angry as the Holy One. His anger is not a capricious emotional outburst in itself. From a theological point of view his anger is directly related to his holiness. God's holiness and jealousy can be expressed as anger. God asserts his rights and does not tolerate his honour being injured. He is not passive when the covenant is broken by his people, nor when Israel's judgement is at hand.

Besides, there is a strong relationship between God's anger and his love. Some theologians have even described God's anger as a tool of his love, and there is some truth in this. Because he loves Israel so dearly, God can become angry. The preaching of judgement is related to God's election by love: 'You only have I chosen of all the families of the earth; therefore I will punish you for all your sins' (Amos 3:2). The prophets sometimes draw a picture of God's coming judgement in a vivid and horrific way, yet behind this there is a deep inner anxiety and indignation about the sin of the people. When they preach the divine wrath, this is rooted in God's holy love, which is guarding the covenant but is deeply hurt.

God's holy anger does not cast shadows over his love, but is the other side of it. His anger is deeply embedded in the covenant. God is angry because he has rights concerning his people. He is angry because they trespass against his commands. He is angry because he keeps his promise – the covenant had been established and sealed with words of curses and blessings (see Chapter 5). The prophets who announce God's anger are watchers and messengers of the covenant (cf. Jer. 6:16-17). Their preaching of judgement is a call for repentance and originates in God's love, which wants to draw the people back to him.

7.4 Dimensions of God's anger

Objects of God's anger

The first object of God's anger is the people who are the most dear to him: Israel. The very first time the Old Testament speaks about God's anger comes in the passage in which Moses tries to pass on to someone else the call to lead Israel out of slavery in Egypt (Ex. 4:13-14). The God who reveals himself to Israel and makes a covenant with his people cannot be manipulated, nor does he want to dance to someone else's tune. Signs of this are the thunder and lightning at Sinai, the heavy cloud, the sound of trumpets, the smoke and the fire (Ex. 19:16-19). Human beings must stand in awe of him, respect him and sanctify themselves; otherwise his anger will come upon his people (Ex. 19:21-24). When Israel still overindulges itself in idolatrous behaviour after the very making of the covenant, God's anger appears (Ex. 32:10). His anger can be released on the whole of Israel because of the sin of one man, for the people and the individuals are related in a collective way (such as in the story of Achan and Ai, Josh. 7). The Psalms often speak of the individual experience of God's anger: 'O LORD, do not rebuke me in your anger or discipline me in your wrath' (Ps. 38:1; 6:1).

In the period before and during the time of the Babylonian exile God's anger against the nations is often mentioned, not the least in oracles such as Jeremiah 46-51 or Ezekiel 25-32. They are Israel's enemies, foreign rulers who threaten God's people. In earlier times we read about God's anger to other nations as well, as in the story of Sodom and Gomorrah (Gen. 18-19), or in Amos' oracles against the nations (Amos 1-2), in which sometimes God's judgement is proclaimed to the surrounding peoples not because of what they did to Israel, but what they did to each other. Particularly in expectations for the future, God's anger against the nations has a prominent place (see below, 7.5).

The reasons for God's anger

In the Old Testament God's anger is almost always motivated by understandable reasons. The flaming of his anger is closely related to people trespassing against his words for life; it is a reaction to it. God is angry because of Israel's ingratitude in the desert; in the book of Numbers we find a litany of their grumbling and murmuring. 'Now the people complained about their hardships in the hearing of the LORD, and when he heard them his anger was aroused. Then fire from the LORD burned among them and consumed some of the outskirts of the camp' (Num. 11:1). God's anger is his answer to Israel's idolatry: 'So Israel joined in worshipping the Baal of Peor. And the LORD's anger burned against them' (Num. 25:3). Israel encounters God's anger when they do not want to follow the Lord wholeheartedly, but disobediently want to enter the land of Canaan;

the result is that they wander in the desert for forty years (Num. 32:10-15). The prophets declare God's anger as a result of social injustice all over the land (Amos 5:7-12), or of their stubborn disbelief in politics (Hos. 7:11-12). Disdain for God's laws, the breach of his covenant and the violation of his name all stir his anger.

When God is angry with the other nations, this may be for several reasons. Some nations are so involved in blood and violence that God wants to stop it. Jonah is ordered to preach to Nineveh: '...because its wickedness has come up before me' (Jon. 1:2). Whenever a nation which is used by God as an instrument for discipline prides itself, like an axe which raises itself 'above him who swings it' (Is. 10:15), then the 'Light of Israel will become a fire, their Holy One a flame; in a single day it will burn and consume his thorns and his briers' (Is. 10:17). Woe to him who violates the apple of God's eye: 'Pour out your wrath on the nations that do not acknowledge you, on the peoples who do not call on your name. For they have devoured Jacob; they have devoured him completely and destroyed his homeland' (Jer. 10:25).

Hard passages

We saw that God's anger is almost always motivated in an ethical religious way. Sometimes, however, that motivation is lacking. Examples of such 'difficult passages' are found in Exodus 4:24-26 (God tries to kill Moses on his way to Egypt, Sippora circumcises her son and uses the words 'bridegroom of blood'); 2 Samuel 6:7 (God's anger burns on Uzziah for preventing the ark from falling); and 2 Samuel 24:1 (God's anger flames against Israel; he incites David to carry out a census). There are other stories which are not easy to understand, like that of Jacob wrestling at night in Peniel (Gen. 32:22-32) or David's remark to Saul ('If the LORD has incited you against me, then he may accept an offering', 1 Sam. 26:19). Because of this some people speak of 'demonic' elements in the image of God in the Old Testament, but we reject that interpretation. We must bear in mind that some passages may be very brief and are handed down to us as a broken fragment. Furthermore, we must keep in mind that later on in the history of revelation more light is thrown on the relationship between God and evil (see Chapter 1). Finally, in the face of these difficult passages we must acknowledge that our understanding is limited.

7.5 The experience of God's anger

How God's anger becomes reality

God's anger does not flare up quickly. Often there is some delay, some restraint, due to God's patience. Yet, if the people do not listen, God goes one step further. He warns by 'striking'. The result may be very disappointing: 'But the people have not returned to him who struck them, nor have they sought the LORD Almighty' (Is. 9:13). Therefore 'his anger is not turned away, his hand is still upraised' (this is the refrain in Is. 9:12,17,21; 10:4; see also 5:25). The prophet Amos has the same sort of bitter refrain. Despite the disciplinary 'striking' it is repeated again and again: '...yet you have not returned to me, declares the LORD' (Amos 4:6,8-11). 'Therefore this is what I will do to you, Israel, and because I will do this to you, prepare to meet your God, O Israel' (Amos 4:12). When God is angry, he turns away his face (2 Chr. 30:9) or he hides it (Ps. 13:1). How destructive can God's anger be in action (Deut. 6:15), when he uses other, hostile nations as his instrument (thus in Is. 10:5 Assyria is called 'the rod of my anger'), or when he uses drought, illness, or the hardening of their hearts (Is. 6:9-10).

The expectation of God's anger

In the historical books of the Old Testament God's anger is often pictured as a disciplinary intervention which takes place from time to time. In the preaching of the prophets the message of God's anger becomes even more serious and threatening. It is not an incident any more, but a reality which becomes permanent: God rages against his people. The prophets have to fight against the false feelings of security and assurance of salvation in Israel, which thinks it is elected and therefore invulnerable. The prophets, however, shed light on the whole of Israel's history and summarize it as a continuous backsliding from God (read for instance Ezek. 16 and 23). Israel did not want to listen. So far God has delayed judgement by his 'striking' and by the preaching of doom. He wanted to bring them back to the heart of the covenant. Yet God's patience is nearly over, they are on the verge of disaster. Jeremiah 'sees' the earth as being 'formless and empty': creation will be destroyed (Jer. 4:23-29).

The prophets repeatedly preach the Day of the Lord. The people of Israel thought that day to be a time of deliverance, when their enemies would be defeated. Yet Amos opens the people's eyes: 'Woe to you who long for the day of the LORD! Why do you long for the day of the LORD? That day will be darkness, not light' (5:18). He already sings the litany of the dead: 'Fallen is Virgin Israel, never to rise again, deserted in her own land, with no one to lift her up' (5:2). Zephaniah names this day 'the day of the LORD's wrath' (2:2) and he calls the people to repent. His description of the great Day of the Lord, which is near, is impressive (1:14-18). In the future the day of the Lord will include judgement on all the nations: 'Therefore wait for me, declares the LORD, for the day I will stand up to testify. I have decided to assemble the nations, to gather the kingdoms and to pour out my wrath on them – all my fierce anger. The whole world will be consumed by the fire of my jealous anger' (Zeph. 3:8; see Is. 13:9-11). Like the dawning of a new day after a dark night, a promise of salvation follows: the vision of a great celebration (Zeph. 3:19-20).

Turning away God's anger

In all sorts of words and nuances the prophets proclaim God's anger to be near. Their aim is that the people may escape from it. Therefore the prophetic preaching is closely related to the call for repentance and confession of sin. The surrounding nations had several instruments to turn away divine anger: incantations, rituals and magic, manipulations in sacrificing. This route is not open to Israel. The essential thing is a broken heart. Intercession and prayer have a special place. God is the One who listens and may change by pleading (for instance in Ex. 32:11-14), although he sometimes forbids intercession (Jer. 7:16; 14:11-12). We also read that God's anger is turned away, because 'her sin has been paid for' (Is. 40:2) or expiation has taken place (Lev. 17:11; 2 Sam. 21:14). The most important reasons for turning away God's anger are based on who he essentially is, and not on what human beings do (see Chapter 9).

7.6 God's anger in the Old and the New Testaments

The key-note of the New Testament

Nowhere in the New Testament is God's anger disapproved of or relegated to the background because of God's love. In the proclamations of John the Baptist, Jesus Christ and the apostles, the idea of God's anger cannot be removed. John the Baptist fulminates against the Pharisees and the Sadducees: 'You brood of vipers! Who warned you to flee from the coming wrath?' (Mt. 3:7). In contrast with the dead orthodoxy, Jesus speaks in anger (Mk. 3:5). Deeply moved and angry in spirit, Jesus stands at the grave of Lazarus (Jn. 11:33,38). Jesus warns about the anger which will strike human beings, if they do not heed the call to believe and repent (Mt. 18:34-35; 22:13; 25:12; 25:26-30). Who can survive in the great day of the Lamb's anger (Rev. 6:16-17)?

Jesus Christ died and rose from the dead: this very message of the Gospel opened the eyes of the apostles to the immense reality of God's anger and wrath. All of the world's history is dominated by God's love (Jn. 3:16) *and* by God's anger (Jn. 3:36; Rom. 1:18). By nature, all human beings are children of wrath, dead because of their sins (Eph. 2:5). God is a 'consuming fire' (Heb. 10:29-31; 12:29), he already lets us feel his wrath (Rom. 3:5). The Gospel of Jesus Christ saves us from the coming wrath (1 Thes. 1:10), because Christ endured God's judgement for all those who belong to him; he drank the cup (Mt. 26:39,42). Not only the love of Christ urges Paul to call for reconciliation (2 Cor. 5:14), but also the knowledge of how much God is to be feared (2 Cor. 5:11). God's patience delays the manifestation of his anger to all godless people, in order that they may repent (Rom. 2:4). God does not want any to perish (2 Pet. 3:9).

The New Testament preachers understand that God's love and his anger are not mutually exclusive, but inclusive. Whenever God's love is despised and crushed, love turns into anger. The reality of God's anger can only be understood as originating from his love. The more one gets to know God's love, the more one fears his anger.

The eternal wrath

Believers in the Old Testament had a restricted view of life after death. In their expectations they almost entirely lacked the dimension of eternity. The same is true of Old Testament texts about God's anger. However fierce and frightening the prophecies about God's wrath may be, there is always the knowledge of God not being angry for ever (Ps. 103:9; Jer. 3:5). Nowhere in the Old Testament do we read about God's 'eternal wrath'. Even when Jeremiah needs to announce exile by saying: 'I will enslave you to your enemies in a land you do not know, for you have kindled my anger, and it will burn for ever' (17:4), it is followed by words like these: 'I will surely gather them from all the lands where I banish them in my furious anger and great wrath; I will bring them back to this place and let them live in safety' (Jer. 32:37). At the end of the Old Testament, however, Malachi speaks of Edom as 'a people always under the wrath of the LORD (KJV: the people against whom the LORD hath indignation for ever)' (1:4). Although the Old Testament concept of eternity has the meaning of a sort of 'endless time', this text in Malachi comes close to what we mean by God's eternal wrath. Edom has become a symbol of powers which are enemies of God and God's anger will not be turned away from them (cf. also Is. 34; Jer. 49:7-22 and Ezek. 35). Similarly there can be no misunderstanding of the end of the book of Daniel, which speaks about two sorts of resurrection: 'Multitudes who sleep in the dust of the earth will awake: some to everlasting life, others to shame and everlasting contempt' (12:2).

In the person and work of Jesus Christ, God's history of revelation reaches its climax. In him God's love reveals itself in such an overwhelming way that the consequences of denying it become all the more clear. The use of the word 'remains' in Jesus' appeal is striking: 'Whoever believes in the Son has eternal life, but whoever rejects the Son will not see life, for God's wrath remains on him' (Jn. 3:36, cf. 12:46). The Saviour speaks about the fire of hell, which 'never goes out' (Mk. 9:43) and is 'eternal' (Mt. 25:41). The book of Revelation pictures reality as an endless 'torment' (14:11; 20:10). The definitive end to all people without God is 'the fiery lake of burning sulphur. This is the second death' (Rev. 21:8). That is why the final words of the Bible are clearly warning and appealing in an emotional way; they invite without restriction: 'The Spirit and the bride say, "Come!" And let him who hears say, "Come!" Whoever is thirsty, let him come; and whoever wishes, let him take the free gift of the water of life' (Rev. 22:17).

Questions

1. What is the main difference between human anger and God's anger, and between the anger of the Ancient Near Eastern gods and that of Israel's God?

2. What exactly do we mean when we state that God's anger is a reality, but not essential?

3. Compare 2 Samuel 24:1 with 1 Chronicles 21:1 and discuss the difference between the passages.

4. Is it possible that we experience something of God's anger in our lives as well, and if so, how?

5. Throughout the centuries there have been scholars who have questioned the reality of eternal wrath and death. They hope that hell is a sort of purifying process, so that all things will be well at the end. What do you think is the background of their ideas and how can we evaluate them?

Bibliography

Baloian, B.E., *Anger in the Old Testament*, Claremont 1992.

Erlandsson, S., 'The Wrath of YHWH', *Tyndale Bulletin* 23 (1973), 111-116.

Hanson, A.T., *The Wrath of the Lamb*, London 1957.

Haney, H.M., *The Wrath of God in the Former Prophets*, New York 1960.

Koch, K. (ed.), *Um das Prinzip der Vergeltung in Religion und Recht des Alten Testaments* (Wege der Forschung 125), Darmstadt 1972.

Morris, L., 'The Wrath of God', *Expository Times* 63 (1952), 142-145.

Tasker, R.V.G., *The Biblical Doctrine of the Wrath of God*, London 1951.

Travis, S.H., *Christ and the Judgment of God. Divine Retribution in the New Testament*, Basingstoke 1986.

Volz, P., *Das Dämonische in Jahwe*, Tübingen 1924.

8

God's Holiness in the Old Testament

8.1 The concept of holiness

'Holy' and 'saint'

In modern language the words 'holy' and 'holiness' can be used in all sorts of different ways. We speak of the 'holy see' (the papal throne), the 'holy' war of Islamic fundamentalists, having a 'holy fear' of someone. We speak of a 'plaster saint' who in fact is a hypocrite. Everyone knows that by the word 'holy' something special is meant, something to respect, which must not be defiled. In the Roman-Catholic and Anglican traditions the word is used very often. When one goes on holiday to France, which used to be a mainly Catholic country, one comes across a lot of place names which start with 'Saint' or 'Sainte' (usually abbreviated to St). The Roman church has declared many people to be 'saints'. We all know names like St Andrew, St Martin and St Patrick. People prefer to reserve the word 'holy' for very special persons, but in doing so they lean more towards the Catholic than the biblical way of speaking.

History of religion

It is clear that not only the Bible and Christianity use the word holiness. It is generally used in all religions. Each one has some idea of the 'other world', which may be felt in ours. In all religions a distinction is made between holy and profane or common. In religious studies much has been written about the concept of holiness. Some scholars have even found this to be the most significant element of the phenomenon of 'religion'. World-famous is Rudolph Otto's book *Das Heilige* (Breslau, 1917, many reprints; first English translation in 1923). Otto describes the mental reactions of human beings on encountering the holy. It awakens emotions in humans which are contrasting and harmonious at the same time: on the one hand they fear and tremble, on the other hand they feel attracted to the holy. It is therefore a mystery which is both frightening and fascinating. In religious studies parallels are drawn between the Melanesian concept of mana and the Polynesian idea of *tabu*. *Mana* is the holy as a mysterious power, present in all sorts of things. It may be a danger or a blessing. *Tabu* is something one should always beware of; it designates holy powers which are negative. These parallels are interesting, yet they cannot really explain the essence of the way in which the Old Testament speaks of the holiness of God and man.

Nuances of the word 'holy' in the Old Testament

The Old Testament knows different words to indicate the highly charged life situation of the encounter of the divine and the human. Humankind lives in the area of tension, on the border between 'holy' and 'profane/unholy', 'clean' and 'unclean' – all of these indicating the nuances of the concept of holiness. It is the

priests' task to show the way in this area of tension, therefore they are forbidden to drink wine or other fermented
drinks whenever they go into the Tent of Meeting: 'This
is a lasting ordinance for the generations to come. You
must distinguish between the holy and the common,
between the unclean and the clean, and you must teach
the Israelites all the decrees the LORD has given them
through Moses' (Lev. 10:10-11). Ezekiel reproaches the
priests for violating God's law and defiling holy things:
'...they do not distinguish between the holy and the common; they teach that there is no difference between the
unclean and the clean...' (22:26). We come across a specific case of teaching the law concerning holy/unholy,
clean/unclean in Haggai 2:11-14, where the prophet is
presenting a matter of detail to the priests.

There have been many discussions about the original
meaning of the word 'holy'. Some scholars derived the
word from a root which means 'splendour, radiance,
brightness'. Others are probably more correct when they
derive the word from the root 'to separate'. Holy is that
which is separated from the ordinary things, from the
'profane'. Read for instance Leviticus 20:26, where God
says to Israel: 'You are to be holy to me because I, the
LORD, am holy, and I have set you apart from the nations
to be my own.' Being holy has both a negative and a positive aspect: to be separated from the profane and from
sin, and to be dedicated to God. Holiness always
includes separation (cf. Ezek. 42:20).

8.2 God is totally different

Incomparable

In a unique way the Old Testament proclaims that God
is the Holy One. He is incomparable and cannot just be

included in our usual, human, way of thinking and experience. Maybe the best way to express that God is the Holy One is by calling him the 'wholly other One', the One who is totally different. This is deeply embedded in Israel's faith. At the Sea of Reeds, at the beginnings of her history, Israel sang this song: 'Who among the gods is like you, O LORD? Who is like You – majestic in holiness, awesome in glory, working wonders?' (Ex. 15:11). And Hannah sings: 'There is no one holy like the LORD; there is no one besides you; there is no Rock like our God' (1 Sam. 2:2). God, 'the Holy One' himself, speaks the following words: 'To whom will you compare me? Or who is my equal?' (Is. 40:25).

Of course, in the surrounding world people spoke of the holiness of gods, human beings and things as well. In this respect, there is a certain similarity between all religions. However, several Old Testament scholars have pointed to the fact that there is a big difference between Israel and the surrounding nations. Everything in the Old Testament is put in a new light, that of the enormous splendour of God's holiness in a very personal way. God, by his holy word, takes a claim to all aspects of human life. In Israel only the LORD is completely 'holy'. All other things and people are holy in so far as they belong to him. In the surrounding world the concept of holiness is not used for gods in such an extensive way, but all sorts of different things, times, places, objects, etc., are charged with holiness in an impersonal, almost magical way.

An essential feature

In a special way, holiness is a characteristic of the God of the Bible. We agree with Theodoor Vriezen (*An Outline of Old Testament Theology*, Oxford 1958) that holiness is the main characteristic of the Old Testament belief in God.

No other concept reveals so much about who God really is, neither is any other attribute of God used so often. God's holiness penetrates all his other 'qualities' or 'virtues'. His love is holy love, his anger is holy anger, his compassion is holy compassion. He is holy, the One who is totally different. How impressed are human beings who encounter the word of God, and the Holy One?

8.3 God's holiness as a source of fear

God's holiness marks the infinite distinction

In the first place, God's holiness means that he is totally different from all creation. 'For I am God, and not man – the Holy One among you' (Hos. 11:9). His holiness means unapproachability and marks the infinite, frightening distance between God and humankind. Its effect is that people bow down; they are tongue-tied, and convinced of their own futility. God's holiness frightens human beings in their inner self. Isaiah 6, the call of the prophet, is illustrative. In this passage even the angels are hiding their face before the holy God (v. 2). Isaiah hears the angels' song: 'Holy, holy, holy is the LORD Almighty; the whole earth is full of his glory' (v. 3), and he cries: 'Woe to me! ... I am ruined! For I am a man of unclean lips, and I live among a people of unclean lips, and my eyes have seen the King, the Lord Almighty' (v. 5). In Psalm 99 the 'trishagion' occurs as well: three times the refrain of the psalm is that the Lord 'is holy' (vv. 3,5,9). This is related to the call to the nations to 'tremble' and to 'shake' (v. 1).

God's name is called 'awesome' (Ex. 15:11; Ps. 111:9). Isaiah receives instructions not to fear or be frightened like the people, but: 'The LORD Almighty is the one you are to regard as holy, he is the one you are to fear, he is the one you are to dread' (Is. 8:13). The implication of this is given in verses 14-15. Salvation will come if Jacob sanctifies the Holy One of Jacob again and stands in awe of him (Is. 29:23). Acknowledging God's holiness and 'standing in awe' of him are synonymous in this passage. It means confessing that he is holy, and acknowledging that there is an absolute contrast between the holy God and the futile, sinful human being. That is why humankind needs to bow before him in deep submission. The encounter with the holy God evokes immediate reaction in human beings, like the people of Beth Shemesh in 1 Samuel 6:20: 'Who can stand in the presence of the LORD, this holy God?' (cf. Ps. 76:7). On meeting the holy God, people fall as dead to the ground (Rev. 1:17).

God's holiness the cause of judgement

God's holiness is a source of fear, and this is not related only to the consciousness of unlimited futility, but also to that of sinfulness, which overcomes humans in the encounter of God's holiness. God is light and in him there is no darkness (1 Jn. 1:5) – when we meet him, we are immediately aware of our own darkness. God is the Holy One, the One who is totally different in his purity and sinlessness. That is why Habakkuk desperately asks himself how it is possible that the Lord, who has always been his God, the Holy One, and who is too pure to see sin or injustice, makes use of an unholy people like the Chaldeans for Israel to be punished (Hab. 1:12-13).

Several times God's holiness becomes apparent in judgement. When God sanctifies himself for the two sons of Aaron, Nadab and Abihu, who brought a foreign fire to the altar, they are consumed by fire (Lev. 10:1-3). At Meriba the Israelites fight with the Lord, and he shows he is the Holy One. This story emerges in judgement on Moses, who is not allowed to bring Israel into the promised land (Num. 20:13). Sometimes we read the expression 'God swears...', which results in the coming of judgement (Amos 4:2; 6:8; cf. also Ps. 89:35). Sin affects God's holiness, and judgement results from God's holy abhorrence of sin.

In Isaiah's prophecy in particular the proclamation of God's holiness plays an important role, from the very beginning of his visionary call (Is. 6). Typical of his message are the words 'the Holy One of Israel'. This name of God, used frequently by the prophet, is in a sense the programme, the main thrust of Isaiah's preaching. The expression 'Holy One of Israel' is almost a paradox! The One who cannot be compared to anyone else has associated himself with a people burdened by sin. The very fact that Israel is God's people and that God is the Holy One of Israel heightens the seriousness of sin and highlights God's grace. Isaiah deals with Israel's turning away from the Holy One of Israel (1:4; 5:24; 30:11; 31:1). Therefore judgement will follow (5:24; 30:12-17; 31:2). At the same time he proclaims that God will leave a 'remnant', and that his holiness will turn against Israel's enemy: 'The Light of Israel will become a fire, their Holy One a flame; in a single day it will burn and consume his Asshur's thorns and his briers' (10:17). Then people 'will rejoice in the Holy One of Israel' (29:19, cf. 10:20; 12:6).

8.4 God's holiness as a source of joy

God living with people

The absolutely elevated holiness of God makes human beings aware of their futility and their sinfulness, and is a source of fear. Yet this does not mean that God's holiness makes a relationship between God and humankind impossible. The holy God wants to be with people. This is striking in Isaiah 57:15: 'For this is what the high and lofty One says – he who lives for ever, whose name is holy: I live in a high and holy place, but also with him who is contrite and lowly in spirit, to revive the spirit of the lowly and to revive the heart of the contrite.' Hosea 11:9 expresses this in a straightforward way: 'For I am God, and not man – *the Holy One among you*' (a passage dealt with before; italics mine). His compassion is overcoming his anger. God's amazing change of heart is based on his holiness. He is totally different, even in his love.

In and around the Babylonian exile in particular the concept of 'holiness' becomes more positive in sound and colour. God in his holiness devotes himself to save his people. The same applies to the concept of 'jealousy', which is closely related to that of holiness. They often appear together (see also Chapter 3). Concerning the idea of God's jealousy as well as his holiness, we can describe a development in usage: from judgement, source of fear (in particular in pre-exilic times), to salvation and source of joy (especially in and after the Babylonian exile).

As an example compare Joshua 24, a passage from the beginnings of Israel's history (thirteenth–twelfth century BC) with Ezekiel 39, a text in the exilic period (following the fall of Jerusalem in 586 BC) and Zechariah 8 from the post-exilic period (about 520 BC). In Joshua 24:19 Joshua says to the people: 'You are not able to serve the LORD. He is a holy God; he is a jealous God. He will not forgive your rebellion and your sins.' Both jealousy and holiness are put in the context of God's frightening judgement of Israel. Yet in Ezekiel 39:25 God announces: 'I will now bring Jacob back from captivity and will have compassion on all the people of Israel, and I will be zealous for my holy name.' In this text God's jealousy and holiness are put into action for the salvation of Israel. The same message occurs in Zechariah 8:2-3:

> This is what the LORD Almighty says: I am very jealous for Zion; I am burning with jealousy for her. This is what the LORD says: I will return to Zion and dwell in Jerusalem. Then Jerusalem will be called the City of Truth, and the mountain of the LORD Almighty will be called the Holy Mountain.

God the holy Deliverer in Deutero-Isaiah; God's holy Name in Ezekiel

In and after the exile this is the way in which the Bible speaks about God's holiness. In his holiness the Lord does not destroy his people. His holiness is a source of joy, comfort and encouragement. This message is heard, particularly in Isaiah 40-55. These chapters are from a prophet who is not mentioned by name, but is known as 'Deutero-Isaiah'. Closely related to the preaching of Isaiah, who prophesied in the last decades of the eighth century bc, Deutero-Isaiah speaks of the holy God as the *Go'el*, the Redeemer. 'Do not be afraid, O worm Jacob, O little Israel, for I myself will help you, declares the LORD, your Redeemer, the Holy One of Israel' (Is. 41:14). The same sort of language is used in Isaiah 43:14; 47:4; 48:17; 49:7; 54:5.

The prophet Ezekiel uses a particular form of speech as well. Constantly he speaks about God's 'holy name' and its 'defilement'. Yet the Lord will sanctify himself, will prove to be the Holy One. He will prevent his name being defiled again (cf. Ezek. 20:39,41; 28:22,25; 38:16; 39:25,27).

For Israel this means redemption. Ezekiel 36:16-27 is illustrative, where the main point is verses 23-24:

> I will show the holiness of my great name, which has been profaned among the nations, the name you have profaned among them. Then the nations will know that I am the Lord, declares the Sovereign Lord, when I show myself holy through you before their eyes. For I will take you out of the nations; I will gather you from all the countries and bring you back into your own land.

Because of this, the Holy One of Israel is praised in the Psalms in every possible way. We confine ourselves to one example: 'In him our hearts rejoice, for we trust in his holy name' (Ps. 33:21, cf. 71:22; 103:1; 145:21).

God's holiness and Israel's expectation for the future

God's holiness plays an important role in Israel's expectation for the future. All its history of judgement and salvation leads to the time when the enemies will suffer for their rebellion against the Holy One of Israel (Is. 47:4; Jer. 50:29; 51:5). Then the ones who remain in Zion, Israel's remnant, shall be called holy (Is. 4:3). At that time the Lord will purify his people through a new covenant, so that they will completely belong to him (Jer. 31). God himself will teach them obedience, so that his holy name will not be defiled any more (Ezek. 20:39-44; 43:7-9). Even the other nations will receive different, pure lips to call upon God's name (Zeph. 3:9, cf. Jes. 6:5-7). More and more a picture of the future arises: there shall be a holy God and a holy nation together, on the day when God's holiness will include everything and nothing profane will be found any more. In a splendid vision the prophet Zechariah saw the following:

> On that day HOLY TO THE LORD will be inscribed on the bells
> of the horses, and the cooking pots in the LORD's house will
> be like the sacred bowls in front of the altar. Every pot in
> Jerusalem and Judah will be holy to the LORD Almighty ...
> And on that day there will no longer be a Canaanite in the
> house of the LORD Almighty (14:20-21).

On the turban of the high priest a plate of gold was
attached with the words: 'Holy to the LORD' (Ex. 28:36).
Zechariah proclaims in different words, by using a striking image, that the time will come when the holy things
will supersede the profane. Even normal objects (bells,
pots) will be as holy as the holy pots and pans of the temple. God will be 'all in all'. His holiness will bring it about.

8.5 God's holiness in Israel's worship

Holy persons, places, times, objects

What is mentioned above brings us to the area of the
cult, Israel worshipping God. God is holy; his word and
will rule over Israel's faith and its religious life.
Everything that belongs to him is holy, that which he
claims or that which one dedicates to him. In the first
place persons can be called holy: the heavenly beings
near to God (Ps. 89:5,7; Job 15:15), believers in general
(Ps. 34:9), the first-born (Ex. 13:2), the prophets (Jer. 1:5),
the priests (Lev. 21:6-24), soldiers in the wars of the Lord
(Josh. 3:5; 1 Sam. 21:5). The people of Israel itself are
called 'a holy nation' (Ex. 19:6; Jer. 2:3). There are also
holy places, of which we mention the Most Holy Place,
the inaccessible area at the back of the temple where God
lives (cf. Ex. 3:5; 19:12; Is. 11:9). We mention also some
holy times, like the Sabbath (Is. 58:13; Ezek. 22:26;

Ex. 31:14-17) and other days of feasting (Lev. 23). Finally, there are holy things, such as the ark of the covenant and the tabernacle, everything which belongs to the temple materials and the clothes of the priests, the sacrifices and the offerings.

Impersonal, material holiness?

To us it seems strange how often certain objects are called 'holy'. Sometimes even touching holy things is sufficient to become 'holy' (Ex. 29:37; 30:29). The holy materials can be touched by Aaron and his sons, yet the Levites who carry the tabernacle will die if they touch the holy things (Num. 4:15,20; cf. Lev. 6:24-30). Compare this with the instructions mentioned above concerning holy and unclean which Haggai receives (Hag. 2:12-14). In passages like these, holiness almost seems to be something impersonal, material, a sort of transferable, electrifying power. Yet this is not the same as a *manu* or *tabu* belief. The Old Testament scholar Gerhard von Rad is right when he remarks that when God stamps things, they belong to him. If anyone violates them, that person is not touched by an inherent, holy sort of power (*manu* or *tabu*), but by God's punishing judgement. In the Old Testament, God claims the whole of life, not only human beings or things. Von Rad states that 'salvation is deeply rooted in the material' (*Old Testament Theology* 1).

8.6 God's holiness and the sanctification of his people

Election and sanctification in Deuteronomy

When the holy God relates to human beings, they must be holy as he is holy. God's holiness requires a holy life, which means that it must be dedicated to him. God is the One who is totally different, so the people who belong to him must be totally different as well. This 'sanctification' includes the banning of all pagan practices – a theme which is particularly stressed in the book of Deuteronomy. Prominent is Deuteronomy 7:6: 'For you are a people holy to the LORD your God. The LORD your God has chosen you out of all the peoples on the face of the earth to be his people...' (cf. Deut. 32:8f.). These words are repeated in Chapter 14 in the context of the command not to make incisions (14:1-2), not to eat carcasses or cook a young goat in its mother's milk (14:21) – each one being a pagan custom. After all, Israel is chosen by God from amongst all the other nations (28:9). Election and sanctification are closely related. Faith and ethics can never be separated.

The law of holiness in Leviticus 17-26

What is mentioned above is still more significant in another Old Testament book in which the law is central: Leviticus (see also Chapter 5.2). Leviticus contains a separate, coherent series of laws which is called 'the Holiness Code': Leviticus 17-26. This name is derived from the central verse 19:2: 'Be holy because I, the LORD your God, am holy.' In all the different areas of life these words are heard, 'I am the LORD, your God'. Combined with the laws on cultic cleanness, the laws on ethical purity are a striking witness to the all-embracing rights of the holy God over his holy people. The everyday life of Israel, however, was often lived far below the level of the laws about holiness. It is at this point that the prophetic preaching of sin and grace, of reconciliation and purification, of renewal and new expectations, starts.

8.7 Holiness and sanctification in the Old and the New Testament

God's Son the Holy One; the Holy Spirit

If we read on from the Old Testament into the New, we notice that many lines of the preaching of God's holiness are continued in a very specific way. In Jesus Christ Hosea 11:9 is full reality: the Holy One amidst his people. He is the Immanuel, God-with-us. He holds the key of David, he opens and no one can shut, he shuts and no one can open – and his name is 'holy and true' (Rev. 3:7). Christ restored his own into a right relationship with God by his death, which brought atonement, and by his resurrection (justification, Rom. 4:25). He brought them peace (Rom. 5:1), but he also becomes 'holiness' for them (1 Cor. 1:30; Eph. 5:26; Heb. 2:11). Through the Holy Spirit this process of sanctification is realized in the life of believers. They do not live any more according to their sinful nature, but according to the Spirit (Rom. 8:4); by the Spirit they 'put to death the misdeeds of the body' (Rom. 8:13).

The church as a holy nation and a holy priesthood

The church is the people of God, composed of Jews and non-Jews, grafted in Israel. The words once spoken to Israel, 'a kingdom of priests and a holy nation' (Ex. 19:6), are from now on also directed to the church (1 Pet. 2:9). God's people are a holy priesthood, a spiritual house in which spiritual sacrifices are made (1 Pet. 2:5). The community of believers is addressed as 'saints' (Rom. 1:7; 1 Cor. 1:2). This does not apply to very special Christians only, to those who are 'advanced' or 'initiated', but to all believers, the great and the small, because they are 'in Christ'.

The place of sanctification in the life of the believer

Sanctification occupies an important place in the life of a bel-iever. The words 'be holy, for I am holy', once spoken to Israel in the Old Testament, are now directed to Christ's church as well: 'As obedient children, do not conform to the evil desires you had when you lived in ignorance. But just as he who called you is holy, so be holy in all you do; for it is written: Be holy, because I am holy' (1 Pet. 1:14-15). No longer are all sorts of materials, times and places holy: all this belongs to the dispensation of 'the shadows' (see the Belgic Confession of Faith, article 25). All the more, in view of the compassion of God in Christ which takes our breath away, believers are urged to bring a living, holy, God-pleasing sacrifice to every aspect of life; this is their 'reasonable worship' (Rom. 12:1). The whole of life becomes worship, not only in the religious aspect, but also socially, sexually, financially, etc. For that purpose God has given the Holy Spirit (1 Thes. 4:8). Indeed, without sanctification no one can meet God; that is why we must make an effort to live in this way (Heb. 12:14).

Expectations for the future; the holy city

Christ Jesus is our holiness. In him the future has already become reality. In the present time, however, the future is not yet fully realized. On the bells of the horses is not yet written 'holy to the LORD' (Zech. 14:20). Yet that day will come, as it is proclaimed for our encouragement, particularly in the book of Revelation. The 'trishagion' from Isaiah shall be sung: 'Holy, holy, holy is the Lord God Almighty, who was, and is, and is to come' (Rev. 4:8). And in the wonderful vision of God's great future the end is the view of the new Jerusalem descending from heaven, the *holy* city (22:19), and the rejoicing that the Lord will be all in all. In the meantime, those who are holy are even more sanctified (22:11), and the perfumery of the saints' prayers goes up to him (8:3-4) who is the only Holy One (15:4).

Questions

1. What are the two aspects of the word 'holy' and what are the implications for our daily life?

2. Suppose you are on a journey to Israel. You travel through Judea's desert. On your way, you go for a walk and you notice how a Bedouin boy throws some pebbles into one of the numerous caves ... where he discovers the ark of the covenant from the temple of Solomon. It has been hidden there for ages. You run towards it. Would you dare to touch the ark of God (cf. Num. 4:15)?

3. In what way can God's holiness be a source of fear even after Christ's coming ?

4. What is the meaning of the phrase 'Christ is our holiness' (1 Cor. 1:30)?

5. What role does the idea of holiness play in our expectation for the future?

Bibliography

Bonar, H., *God's Way of Holiness*, Hertfordshire 1979.
Gammie, J.G., *Holiness in Israel*, Minneapolis 1989.

Hänel, J., *Die Religion der Heiligkeit*, Gütersloh 1931.

Hubbard, R.L. (ed.), *Studies in Old Testament Theology. Historical and Contemporary Images of God and God's People*, Dallas 1992.

Milgrom, J., *Studies in Cultic Theology and Terminology*, Leiden 1983.

Peels, H.G.L., *Heilig is zijn Naam. Onze godsbeelden en de God van de Bijbel*, Bedum 2000.

Peels, H.G.L., 'Heiligheid en heiliging in de oudtestamentische eschatologie', in: C.J. van den Boogert and G.C. den Hertog (eds.), *Hedendaagse zoektocht naar heiligheid. Aspecten van heiligheid in de Bijbel en in de joodse en christelijke traditie*, Kampen 1999, 35-51.

von Rad, G., *Old Testament Theology 1*, 7th impr., Woking 1996.

Snaith, N.H., *The Distinctive Ideas of the Old Testament* (1944), repr. Carlisle 1997.

Trevethan, Th.L., *The Beauty of God's Holiness*, Downers Grove 1995.

Wright, D.P., 'Holiness (OT)' in: *The Anchor Bible Dictionary. Volume 3*, New York 1992, 237-249.

9

God's Forgiveness in the Old Testament

9.1 Who is like you?

The other side of the question

In our preface we referred to Moses' song in Exodus 15. Full of awe, Israel sings at the Sea of Reeds: 'Who among the gods is like you, O LORD? Who is like you – majestic in holiness, awesome in glory, working wonders?' (Ex. 15:11). From the immediate context it is clear that this question rises from a deep awareness of God's anger and punishing force over his enemies: 'Your right hand, O LORD, was majestic in power. Your right hand, O LORD, shattered the enemy' (v. 6). Who of the gods, who are essentially dumb, deaf and blind (Is. 44:6-20), can be compared with him? In this study we dealt with several aspects of God's terrifying majesty, with the 'shadow sides' of God's revelation in the Old Testament. Through a closer look, we noticed again and again that these 'shadow sides' did not deny but rather stressed the light of God's revelation. God's terrifying intervention is not isolated, but serves a definite purpose. The question 'Who is like you?' has two aspects: people both tremble

at God's punishing hand and are joyful because of
his saving hand. 'You stretched out your right hand and
the earth swallowed them. In your unfailing love you
will lead the people you have redeemed. In your
strength you will guide them to your holy dwelling'
(Ex. 15:12-13).

In the same way the author of Psalm 35 says: 'Then
my soul will rejoice in the LORD and delight in his salvation. My whole being will exclaim, Who is like you, O
LORD? You rescue the poor from those too strong for
them, the poor and needy from those who rob them' (vv.
9-10). The other, positive side of the question 'Who is like
you?' did not get much attention in this survey, because
of the themes dealt with; yet we want to finish this book
by discussing it. God can hide himself, he can be jealous
or repent, he avenges in holy anger, yet he is first of all
the One who turns to human beings with great compassion and loves to forgive. Thus we search for the Old
Testament message of God's forgiveness after our deal-
ings with the terminology and concept of God's punishing *retribution*.

The essence of forgiveness

In the first place we need to give a definition of 'forgiveness'. In simple words we mean the expiation of guilt.
Guilt is always caused by sin. Guilt requires forgiveness,
remission, absolution, amnesty, justification, reconciliation. Through forgiveness guilt is wiped out from mem-
ory and does not exist any more before God. The value
of forgiveness is immense. Through forgiveness the relationship with God, which was disturbed by sin, is
restored. Forgiveness builds a bridge over a deep gap; it
opens doors which were hermetically sealed, it renews
and changes what was hurt.

That is why the author of Psalm 32 does not lose himself in theoretical reflections, but pronounces a blessing: 'Blessed is he whose transgressions are forgiven, whose sins are covered. Blessed is the man whose sin the LORD does not count against him...' (vv. 1-2). Forgiveness is always coloured by grace. We cannot claim it, yet we may ask for it in great expectation, holding on to the promises and commitment of God, who is explicitly called in the Old Testament the 'God of forgiveness' (Neh. 9:17). Without the reality of forgiveness life cannot be lived and death would only be the passage to eternal death.

Expressions and metaphors for forgiveness in the Bible

Which terms and metaphors does the Old Testament use to express the concept of forgiveness? Of course we mention in the first place the word 'forgive' itself (Num. 14:20). It is striking that it occurs as many times in the Old Testament as in the New. In the second place there is the expression 'to make atonement' (Ezek. 16:63), which indicates the covering of guilt. In the third place words related to 'compassion' are often used (Lam. 3:32): God turns to humans in his grace, in compassion, in lovingkindness. In the fourth place we often read that God is 'coming to' humans (Jer. 29:10), which implies the initiating of the act of forgiveness and deliverance. In the fifth place, God 'takes away, lifts off' guilt (translated as 'forgive' in Ex. 34:7). And finally, God does not 'remember' guilt any more (Jer. 31:34). There are still some other, less frequently used words. The Old Testament has a great variety of words to express the immense richness of forgiveness.

Forgiveness may be phrased in a very expressive, striking way. For instance the metaphor of healing is used: 'Praise the LORD, O my soul, and forget not all his benefits – who forgives all your sins and heals all your diseases' (Ps. 103:2-3, cf. Is. 57:17-18). Then there is the metaphor of cleaning thoroughly, of cleansing:

> Have mercy on me, O God, according to your unfailing love; according to your great compassion blot out my transgressions. Wash away all my iniquity and cleanse me from my sin ... Cleanse me with hyssop, and I shall be clean; wash me, and I shall be whiter than snow (Ps. 51:1-2,7).

Perhaps the prophet Micah uses the most expressive metaphors by confessing in a song at the end of his book (7:18-19):

> Who is a God like you, who pardons sin and forgives the transgression of the remnant of his inheritance? You do not stay angry forever but delight to show mercy. You will again have compassion on us; you will tread our sins underfoot and hurl all our iniquities into the depths of the sea.

What a marvellous hymn and confession! We notice in it a certain climax: 1. God forgives (the RSV reads that he is 'passing over transgression'); 2. God will 'tread the sins underfoot' (he crushes them, so to speak); and 3. God is throwing sins into the depths of the sea (no one can ever see the guilt again). That is what forgiveness is about: God is throwing away guilt into the sea, never to remember it again.

9.2 Forgiveness is characteristic of the Lord

God's forgiveness in the torah

In our reflections on the 'shadow sides' of God's revelation in the Old Testament we frequently encountered the misunderstanding in church history that the Old Testament deals with justice and revenge and the New Testament with love, that the Old Testament mainly preaches revenge and the New Testament forgiveness. When we read the Scriptures honestly, we see again and again that this opinion cannot stand up. The Old Testament makes clear that forgiveness is characteristic of Israel's God. We will deal with this briefly, dividing the Old Testament in the Jewish way: the *torah* or Law (Genesis – Deuteronomy), the Prophets (Joshua – Kings and Isaiah – Malachi) and the Writings (the remaining books of the Old Testament).

God's will to forgive is revealed immediately at the beginning of the history of humankind. He provides clothes to cover Adam's and Eve's shame (Gen. 3). He gives Cain a sign to protect him (Gen. 4). In the relationship between God and his people it is through his forgiveness that the history of salvation is not finished. God gives the institution of atonement by ordering sin and guilt offerings to be brought to the sanctuary to reconcile the Israelites (Leviticus). After the people sinned by making the golden calf Moses prays for God's forgiveness and he forgives (Ex. 32:32, also Num. 14:20). When Moses asks to see God's glory, he promises to pass by in his majesty calling out the name of the Lord: 'I will have mercy on whom I will have mercy, and I will have compassion on whom I will have compassion' (Ex. 33:19). When this happens (Ex. 34:6-7), the words compassionate, gracious and slow to anger are heard.

God's forgiveness in the Prophets

Based on the *torah*, the prophets speak about God as the One who forgives. Their preaching of judgement is never so dark that they do not point to the possibility of escaping it by finding a shelter with the God of grace. In Isaiah 55:7 the prophet calls the wicked to turn to the Lord, because then 'he will have mercy on him ... for he will freely pardon'. The same message is given in the so-called Book of Comfort in Jeremiah (Jer. 30-31), when he prophesies that one day God will write the law in the hearts of humans and that they will know him from the least to the greatest: 'For I will forgive their wickedness and will remember their sins no more' (Jer. 31:34). And when the big Adversary holds the trumps to accuse God's people – Joshua, the high priest who represents Israel, is clothed with dirty clothes – even then God holds on to Israel, as 'a burning stick snatched from the fire' (Zech. 3:1-3). This is only possible because of God's most surprising act of forgiveness: 'See, I have taken away your sin, and I will put rich garments on you' (v. 4). God's forgiveness of the people is symbolized by the removal of the dirty clothes and their replacement with a clean garment and a clean turban (vv. 4-5).

God's forgiveness in the Writings

In the Writings we hear no other message. From one psalm to another people call to the Lord as One who is full of grace. 'You are forgiving and good, O Lord...' (Ps. 86:5). People know from deep within: 'If you, O LORD, kept a record of sins, O LORD, who could stand? But with you there is forgiveness; therefore you are feared' (Ps. 130:3-4). The last phrase is the foundation and the cause of high expectations: 'He himself will redeem Israel from all their sins' (Ps. 130:8). Daniel prays: 'O Lord, listen! O Lord, forgive!' (Dan. 9:19), because the Lord is 'merciful and forgiving' (Dan. 9:9).

The Lord is the God to whom people can appeal, however great their guilt. With him is the source of life, thanks to his forgiveness. That is the continuing message of the Old and the New Testaments. Voltaire, one of the philosophers of the Enlightenment, said about God in a mocking way: *'Pardonner, c'est son métier'* (to forgive, that is his job). How much he misunderstood the biblical message, perhaps deliberately, in his mockery. There is nothing self-evident or automatic in the forgiveness of God. It is characteristic of him to such an extent that man can only worship God in deep amazement and reverence. We will discover that even more when we try to describe the motivation of God's forgiveness.

9.3 The motivation of God's forgiveness

Compassion

The Old Testament proclamation of God's forgiveness is multi-faceted and multiform. Many times we read that human beings turn to God in prayer, bringing sacrifices to invoke his forgiveness. Also human repentance and God's forgiveness are interrelated; refusing to repent blocks the possibility to forgive. Often the assurance of forgiveness is linked to the condition of repentance. Yet again and again it is clear that the deepest motivation of forgiveness is found in God himself. Not human initiative but divine grace is decisive. Why does God forgive when human beings pray to him, bring sacrifices, repent, call out, or when they do not do any of these things? What are the most important motives of God's forgiveness? On a closer look, we can discern four motives.

In the first place God is compassionate about the suffering and misery of his people. The Old Testament testifies with emphasis that God sees the troubles of those who are his, in particular of those who are helpless and weak. God sees the misery of Israel in Egypt, groaning in slavery (Ex. 2:23-25; 3:7,9). In the times of the judges he reacts to their crying out because of all the oppressors (Judg. 2:18; 10:16). Nehemiah prays: '...do not let all this hardship seem trifling in your eyes...' (Neh. 9:32). Many writers of the psalms point to their troubles and even sometimes picture them very extensively, to bring God to return (for instance in Psalm 38). The prophet Amos pleads twice on behalf of Israel: 'Sovereign LORD, forgive! How can Jacob survive? He is so small!' (Amos 7:2,5). And the Lord repented. Maybe we read in Isaiah 63:9, a difficult text, that in all Israel's oppression God himself was oppressed. This indicates that God may be most involved in the ups and downs of his people.

However, the reference to misery and need cannot be interpreted as an excuse to take away judgement, but indicates God's deep compassion for a world that suffers and that he did not create in such a state. In particular, this applies to those who belong to him: 'But you, O God, do see trouble and grief; you consider it to take it in hand' (Ps. 10:14). Strikingly, the Psalms often refer to the shortness and mortality of human existence. 'Turn, O LORD, and deliver me; save me because of your unfailing love. No one remembers you when he is dead. Who praises you from his grave?' (Ps. 6:4-5; 30:9). We even read that God turns away his anger because he remembers that human beings are flesh, 'a passing breeze that does not return' (Ps. 78:39).

Loyalty to the covenant

The second inner motivation of God's forgiveness is his loyalty to the covenant. In the Old Testament the relationship between God and his people is expressed by the concept of covenant. That covenant is based on election

(Deut. 7:7) and is maintained by God in 'lovingkind-ness'. Often, therefore, God's forgiveness is introduced by mentioning his remembrance of the covenant. This may apply to his covenant with the patriarchs, the Sinaitic covenant, or the Davidic one. Again and again in the Old Testament, God's steadfast loyalty to the covenant proves able to bridge the gap between today's human guilt and trouble and future restoration and renewal. It happens even when the gap could not be bridged because Israel broke the covenant and God rejected them by sending them into exile (Lev. 26:40-43). The rejection of Israel was not definitive and complete, however – it was temporary. The fact that God can remember his covenant in this way and returns though that seems to be impossible, indicates that there are even deeper motives than simply his loyalty to the covenant.

The honour of God's name

This brings us to the third motive of God's forgiveness in the Old Testament: he is standing up for the honour of his name. God's name would be profaned by the slander of nations which – looking at Israel's destruc-tion – say: 'You see, the God of Israel is powerless and unreliable.' That is why God refrains from his anger and forgives, because he 'dreads' the scorn of the enemies (Deut. 32:26-27) and he does not want his name to be 'profaned' (Ezek. 20:22). In particular those who preach in the times of the Babylonian exile emphasize the words 'for my own name's sake'. 'For my own name's sake I delay my wrath; for the sake of my praise I hold it back from you, so as not to cut you off ... For my own sake, for my own sake, I do this. How can I let myself be defamed? I will not yield my glory to another' (Is. 48:9,11; cf. 43:25).

In a unique way Ezekiel proclaims God's majesty and the honour of his glory: 'It is not for your sake, O house of Israel, that I am going to do these things, but for the sake of my holy name, which you have profaned among the nations where you have gone' (Ezek. 36:22,32; 20:9,14). God is motivated by his innermost being, for his thoughts are higher than ours (Is. 55:9): 'For I know the plans I have for you, declares the LORD, plans to prosper you and not to harm you, plans to give you hope and a future' (Jer. 29:11).

Mercy triumphs over judgement

Now we get to the fourth inner motive of God's forgiveness: his boundless love for his people. When we look at the way in which the Old Testament speaks about it, we may call this the very deepest motive. We remark that in the very passages which preach God's forgiveness based on his mighty love, the image of parental love is frequently used.

Nowhere is the proclamation of mercy which triumphs over judgement more touching than in Hosea 11 (this passage was dealt with in Chapter 4, on the repentance of God). How much God loved his child, his son, Israel: he called him out of Egypt, carried him in his arms, led him with ties of love, taught him how to walk and fed him (vv. 1-4). However, the child walked away permanently – therefore the announced judgement is irreversible and definitive (vv. 5-7). Yet in verses 8-9 we suddenly read about an unexpected, amazing turn: 'How can I give you up, Ephraim? How can I hand you over, Israel?' God cannot execute the deserved judgement which would hit Israel in the same way as that which destroyed the cities of Admah and Zeboiim. 'My heart turns around against me' (my translation). It is not

Israel which is overturned, but a turn takes place in
God's own heart. God's 'repentance', his 'compassion', is
aroused. God does not carry out his fierce anger: he cannot and does not want to cancel Ephraim's calling and
election. 'For I am God, and not man – the Holy One
among you' (v. 9b). Considering God's change and forgiveness, each comparison with human feelings,
thoughts or acts falls short.

The proclamation of Jeremiah 31 can be understood
along the same lines. God has loved his people with an
'everlasting love' (v. 3), as verse 9 says: '...because I am
Israel's father, and Ephraim is my firstborn son.' When
Ephraim humbles itself (vv. 18-19), God cries out (v. 20):
'Is not Ephraim my dear son, the child in whom I
delight? Though I often speak against him, I still remember him. Therefore my heart yearns for him; I have great
compassion for him...' The Hebrew word for heart
literally means 'intestines', and the word 'yearn for' is
something like 'to be restless' (KJV reads: 'my bowels are
troubled for him'). It means a violent inner movement
within the Lord. His forgiveness is based on what lives
deep within him.

Isaiah 63:15 takes up those two words from Jeremiah
31:20 and asks for God's turn by appealing to his inner
compassion, because God is the Father and Redeemer
from of old (v. 16, cf. 64:8). Another significant turn is
found in another passage of Isaiah, 42:18 – 43:8. Isaiah 42
finishes with the lowest point of Israel's total hardening
and the exile, whereas Isaiah 43 starts with the proclamation of God's compassion: 'Since you are precious and
honoured in my sight, and because I love you' (v. 4). The
amazing turn is caused by God's incredible love for a
people which turned away from him – yet it is called by
his name (43:7). Then God's calling voice flashes to all
quarters of the world: 'Bring my sons from afar and my

daughters from the ends of the earth...' (43:6). The Israelites are meant here, those who at the end of the prophecy are still without any trace of repentance and are characterized as 'blind' and 'deaf' (43:8, using the same words as the first verse of the prophecy, 42:18).

9.4 Forgiveness and retribution

Contrast or complement

Forgiveness and retribution, love and revenge, in our eyes are easily regarded as two totally contrasting things. To forgive seems to be a matter of the heart, revenge that of a stern hand. Yet we must be careful to avoid a false contrast. The Old Testament differs from our modern way of speech in regarding forgiveness and retribution, revenge and love, as a complementary and not a contrasting pair of words. On the one hand God's revengeful retribution has nothing to do with an unreliable, cruel, resentful passion to destroy. On the other hand God's forgiving love is not absorbed by indulgence or sensibility, but it may be expressed in anger and jealousy; God's love is dynamic and holy. The one thing does not exist without the other. In this study much is said about 'shadow sides' like God's jealousy and revenge, his anger and his punishing hand. In our research we saw something of the height and depth, width and length of God's revelation in the Old Testament. We stated that the multicoloured language of God's revenge is deeply rooted in the Old Testament preaching about God and the relationship between him and humankind. The 'shadow sides' are not a strange element in the Old Testament. Both God's forgiveness and his revenge are a reality.

Two-sided revelation

In this respect it is very important to keep constantly in mind how God reveals himself. God's revelation in the Bible can be called two-sided. That is most obvious in the rich text Exodus 34:6-7, where God himself says:

> The LORD, the LORD, the compassionate and gracious God, slow to anger, abounding in love and faithfulness, maintaining love to thousands, and forgiving wickedness, rebellion and sin. Yet he does not leave the guilty unpunished; he punishes the children and their children for the sin of the fathers to the third and fourth generation.

These words are frequently recalled in the Old Testament in a variety of ways, for instance in Jonah 4:2, Joel 2:13, Psalm 86:15, 103:8, 145:8, and Nehemiah 9:17. In these words there are two sides of the covenant which constantly return through the whole Bible; two ways (narrow and wide), the curses and the blessings, death and life (Deut. 30). The God of the covenant has revealed himself as a God of grace *and* as One who punishes those who are guilty, bearing in mind the priority of 'love' in the list of Exodus 34:6-7. This bilateral attitude towards humankind is obvious throughout the whole Old Testament. The Lord is a God of blessing and curse, of love *and* anger, grace *and* revenge. This is very obvious in Psalm 99:8. In reviewing history the author puts into words a glimpse of the experience which Israel had with the Lord in the course of time: 'O LORD, our God, you answered them; you were to them a forgiving God and an avenging God because of their misdeeds' (my translation). The NIV says: 'though' you have punished their misdeeds, but the Hebrew literally reads: 'a God, forgiving *and* avenging'. This is our God. In his time, in his way, he forgives and avenges. He moves towards his goal with his people and this world.

God's kingship

To clarify the connection between forgiveness and revenge even further, we point to the concept of the kingship of God, which is at the heart of the biblical message. God is King! A good king, who is also judge and warlord, showing before his people love and loyalty, help and support (Prov. 20:28; 31:4-9). On the other hand he sternly judges the wicked (Prov. 20:26; 25:5; Ps. 101). A ruler would not really love his people if he did not care about the fate of his subjects and let the enemy continue unchecked. A government which proclaims humanity but at the same time does not try to stop criminal behaviour is a failure. Love and justice, revenge and forgiveness, may both be expected in the policy of a good ruler. How much more is this the case for the heavenly King, but with him in perfect manner.

9.5 The predominance of love

The seriousness of revenge

Not yet everything is mentioned in what we have said above. Indeed, there is no contrast or conflict between God's revenge and his forgiveness. However, neither is it possible to get the link between these two 'lists' (on the one hand love, forgiveness, goodness, etc., on the other revenge, retribution, jealousy, etc.) in a completely clear and logical pattern as a sort of balanced construction. How could that be done? The proclamation of the living God is constantly beyond our theological constructions and logical reasoning, in particular if they are more and more remote from biblical language itself. Revenge and forgiveness – how do they relate to each other? We want to mention three things, but in a careful way because our human understanding is limited.

In the first place we notice that the seriousness of God's retribution and revenge in the Bible is never affected or diminished by the knowledge of his love. God's forgiveness does not undermine his retribution. The Bible knows of God's great anger, indeed because he is the God of love. In the Old Testament we frequently read that God deliberately does not forgive (Deut. 29:20; Josh. 24:19; Is. 2:9; etc.). Judgement is executed, connections are broken. Neither the Old Testament nor the New give reason to expect 'that it will all be well in the end'. That was the hope of Origen (about ad 185-254), who taught the *apokatastasis toon pantoon*, the ultimate restoration of all things; even the devil, he thought, would one day turn to God. This speculation goes wrong because of the serious way in which the Bible speaks about the 'fear of the Lord' (2 Cor. 5:11).

Longing for forgiveness

At the same time, however, the Old Testament proclaims in an impressive way the supremacy of God's love. In God's revelation love and anger cannot be reversed indiscriminately. Love has priority. There is no strict balance between God's grace and his judgement, his love and his revenge; love is absolutely superior. In God's relationship with human beings anger is a variable, but love a constant. It is striking that the Old Testament speaks about God's 'everlasting' love (Jer. 31:3) or 'everlasting' kindness (Is. 54:8), but not about 'everlasting' anger. The seriousness of *everlasting* death is not yet proclaimed explicitly in the Old Testament, but only in the New. Again and again God reveals himself as the One who approaches humans with love and compassion. That is the first thing he says:

> For a brief moment I abandoned you, but with deep compassion I will bring you back. In a surge of anger I hid my face from you for a moment, but with everlasting kindness I will have compassion on you (Is. 54:7-8).

The author of Psalm 30 confesses in exactly the same way: 'For his anger lasts only a moment, but his favour lasts a lifetime...' (v. 5). The fact that God is not angry 'for ever' provides a strong foundation for the Old Testament believers' pleading, as is clear in many psalms and at the end of the book of Lamentations.

Concerning judgement the prophet states: 'For he does not willingly bring affliction or grief to the children of men' (Lam. 3:33). God does not like the death of the wicked (Ezek. 18:23; 33:11), but likes to show mercy, justice and righteousness (Jer. 9:24; Mic. 7:18). Even if there were only one human being who did justice in Jerusalem, God would have loved to forgive the city: there is nothing he likes better (Jer. 5:1). The strongest preachers of judgement, who were the closest to the execution of judgement, spoke about God's love in the most passionate way: Hosea just before the fall of Samariah in 722 BC, and Jeremiah at the time of the fall of Jerusalem in 586 BC. The God of love is not another, a foreign God, but the God of judgement is the same God.

The cross on Golgotha

Finally this brings us to the cross on Golgotha. All that is said about God's revenge and his forgiveness, about the

Lord who is a God of righteousness *and* love, comes together in the cross of his own Son. It is beyond description what happens when the light of the world is hanging in the darkness of Golgotha. We see the fierce anger of God, in which he shows at the same time the strongest, most powerful love for us. We remember the question: 'Who is like you?' Golgotha shows who God is for human beings like us. And in that place we may begin to understand part of the wonderful Old Testament preaching of the supremacy of God's love. This does not diminish his punishing righteousness. 'Hear, O Israel: The LORD our God, the LORD is one' (Deut. 6:4).

Questions

1. The Lord reveals himself as the God of forgiveness and revenge, in this order in Exodus 34:6-7. Does that have consequences for preaching and evangelism?

2. What assurance does the Old Testament language of God's loyalty to the covenant as one of the motives of his forgiveness give to us?

3. Discuss the 'amazing turn' in Isaiah 42:18 – 43:7. What is the nature of this turn and how does it come into being?

4. How can Deuteronomy 32:27 state that God 'fears' the taunt of the enemy?

5. What do we mean by the 'supremacy' of God's love, and what is not meant by it?

Bibliography

Childs, B.S., *Old Testament Theology in a Canonical Context*, London 1985.

Childs, B.S., *Biblical Theology of the Old and New Testaments. Theological Reflection on the Christian Bible*, London 1992.

Daube, D., Sin, *Ignorance and Forgiveness in the Bible*, London 1960.

Gunneweg, A.H.J., 'Schuld ohne Vergebung?', *Evangelische Theologie* 36 (1976), 2-14.

McKeating, H., 'Divine Forgiveness in the Psalms', *Scottish Journal of Theology* 18 (1965), 69-83.

Peels, H.G.L., *De omkeer van God in het Oude Testament* (Apeldoornse Studies 33), Apeldoorn 1997.

Peels, H.G.L., 'The Kingdom of God in the Old Testament', *In die Skriflig* 35/2 (2001), 173-190.

Stamm, J.J., *Erlösen und Vergeben im Alten Testament*, Bern 1940.

Zenger, E., *Am Fuss des Sinai. Gottesbilder des Ersten Testaments*, Düsseldorf 1993.

Index of Texts Discussed